WHERE THE SPIRIT BREATHES

Biblical Abbreviations

OLD TESTAMENT

Genesis	Gn	Nehemiah	Ne	Baruch	Ba
Exodus	Ex	Tobit	Tb	Ezekiel	Ezk
Leviticus	Lv	Judith	Jdt	Daniel	Dn
Numbers	Nb	Esther	Est	Hosea	Ho
Deuteronomy	Dt	1 Maccabees	1 M	Joel	Jl
Joshua	Jos	2 Maccabees	2 M	Amos	Am
Judges	Jg	Job	Jb	Obadiah	Ob
Ruth	Rt	Psalms	Ps	Jonah	Jon
1 Samuel	1 S	Proverbs	Pr	Micah	Mi
2 Samuel	2 S	Ecclesiastes	Ec	Nahum	Na
1 Kings	1 K	Song of Songs	Sg	Habakkuk	Hab
2 Kings	2 K	Wisdom	Ws	Zephaniah	Zp
1 Chronicles	1 Ch	Sirach	Si	Haggai	Hg
2 Chronicles	2 Ch	Isaiah	Is	Malachi	Ml
Ezra	Ezr	Jeremiah	Jr	Zechariah	Zc
		Lamentations	Lm		

NEW TESTAMENT

Matthew	Mt	Ephesians	Eph	Hebrews	Heb
Mark	Mk	Philippians	Ph	James	Jm
Luke	Lk	Colossians	Col	1 Peter	1 P
John	Jn	1 Thessalonians	1 Th	2 Peter	2 P
Acts	Ac	2 Thessalonians	2 Th	1 John	1 Jn
Romans	Rm	1 Timothy	1 Tm	2 John	2 Jn
1 Corinthians	1 Cor	2 Timothy	2 Tm	3 John	3 Jn
2 Corinthians	2 Cor	Titus	Tt	Jude	Jude
Galatians	Gal	Philemon	Phm	Revelation	Rv

Where the Spirit Breathes

Prayer and Action

Father Marie-Eugene of the Child Jesus, OCD

Translated by
Sister Mary Thomas Noble, OP

ALBA · HOUSE   NEW · YORK
SOCIETY OF ST. PAUL, 2187 VICTORY BLVD., STATEN ISLAND, NEW YORK 10314

Originally published in French by Éditions du Carmel under the title *Au souffle de l'Esprit: Prière et Action.*

Library of Congress Cataloging-in-Publication Data

Marie-Eugène de l'Enfant-Jésus, père, 1894-1967.
[Au souffle de l'Esprit. English]
Where the spirit breathes: prayer and action / Father Marie-Eugene of the Child Jesus; translated by Mary Thomas Noble.
p. cm.
Includes bibliographical references.
ISBN 0-8189-0806-8
1. Christian life — Catholic authors. I. Title.
BX2350.2.M34413 1998
248.4'82 — dc21 97-41210
CIP

Produced and designed in the United States of America by the Fathers and Brothers of the Society of St. Paul, 2187 Victory Boulevard, Staten Island, New York 10314, as part of their communications apostolate.

ISBN: 0-8189-0806-8

Printing Information:

Current Printing - first digit 1 2 3 4 5 6 7 8 9 10

Year of Current Printing - first year shown

1998 1999 2000 2001 2002 2003 2004 2005

Table of Contents

PART TWO — TOWARD
TRANSFORMATION IN LOVE

PART THREE — IN THE GRIP OF THE SPIRIT

Introduction

What is the aim of this book? We will let the author, Father Marie-Eugene of the Child Jesus, speak for himself:

> Our times are thirsting, hungering for God. We can see this hunger for God not only in souls, in eyes, but in all the lecture halls where God is spoken of. For you know as well as I do, this is what they are asking us to do: to talk about God.[1]

All the spoken conferences, collected and transcribed to form this book, bear witness to the theological spirit which animated Father Marie-Eugene's life and teaching.[2] It is this spirit which unifies his teaching on God and the Christian life, prayer and the apostolate.

Father Marie-Eugene speaks almost exclusively about God and the relationship of grace which unites us to God in Christ. Through grace God reveals Himself to us and makes us instruments of His action in the world and channels of His holiness.

Through grace we find complete fulfillment, our dignity as children of God, and our likeness to Christ Jesus.

However, even though Father Marie-Eugene's language is *spiritual and spiritual only*,[3] he emphasizes the way in which all human realities, from the humble everydayness of life to the vast scope of world history, find their meaning and value in this theological light. He invites us to be fully aware of the riches of grace given us by God, to *make an inventory* of them so as to make them our own, and to let our whole life be ruled by them: "It is not only contemplatives who need to be aware of these realities and to think about them. This is for every Christian, all the baptized, all human beings."[4]

The dignity and beauty of the human person in God

Throughout these conferences Father Marie-Eugene contemplates man in the light of his participation in the divine life. Man's origin and destiny are seen, as it were, through the eyes of God:

> In creating us, God saw us at the level of intimacy with Him. If He placed us in the world, it was so that we might return to Him, to the place destined for us in the mystical Body of Christ and in the Trinitarian life of the three divine Persons.[5]

This gaze reveals human beings to themselves and their vocation and dignity as children of God.[6] In order to fulfill his vocation "the Christian must know his dignity."[7]

This dignity finds *its most striking witness* in the holiness to which we are called.[8] It is the source of the most beautiful of obligations: prayer and sanctification, humble submission to the Holy Spirit, witness, and the apostolate. And if it confers on us who are baptized a true "right" to carry out our vocation,[9] it also requires of us an ever increasing faithfulness and love, in order to bring forth the fruits of holiness: "This is a demanding dignity!"[10]

The Christian receives this dignity and beauty through participation in the divine life. Grace implants in every Christian the life and movement which are in God from all eternity. God alone is its source. It is the very beauty of God. This is what Moses contemplated in the vision of the burning bush, what shone upon the face of Christ:

> We contemplate the beauty of God and through this contemplation "we are being changed into His likeness from one degree of glory to another, for this comes from the Lord who is the Spirit."[11]

Father Marie-Eugene invites us therefore from the outset to contemplate the mystery of God, to discover Him as a living Being since, in Christ, we are called to share His life.

Moses' vision of the burning bush on Mount Horeb is the revelation of the movement and life which are in God. Moses is familiar with the transcendence of God. He knows Him to be infinite, inaccessible.

> But what puzzles him is that this transcendent One is in motion. What is this fire, really? It is a symbolic vision, a theophany of God. God is not only inaccessible, transcendent. In addition to this, He is not obscure. No! God is light, and yet more, God is flame, a flame which leaps up, a blazing fire. God is a fire, shooting out sparks, sending forth rays. There He is![12]

Father Marie-Eugene will comment on this description:

> We have the impression that God is in a hurry, so to speak, to reveal something of His nature, when He shows Himself to Moses in the symbol of the burning bush. He is the God of Israel, the mysterious God Whom no one knows, the motionless God of the desert, of the wandering shepherds. He is the God of simplicity.... It is true that God is perfect, infinitely perfect, and transcendent. Quite true. But we have to add to this the idea of movement, of diffusion, of a flame which leaps up and burns without consuming, but burns forever.[13]

God's transcendence is revealed to Moses as movement and life because *God is love.*[14] He is a God who gives Himself. "This movement that Moses grasped, this fire, is a fire of love."[15] The life shown symbolically in fire and flame is the life of the divine Persons, Father, Son and Holy Spirit. It is eternal, like God Himself:

> God will always engender, the Son will always spring forth, the spiration of love will flow between Father and Son unceasingly, forever and ever and ever.... And God is always happy, God is infinitely happy. [...] Peaceful joy, triumphant joy, happiness unmitigated, joy serene....[16]

God revealed Himself to Moses on Mount Horeb in His divine life and transformed him, enriching him with His own being. Jesus proclaimed that He was the unique and true witness of God, and bestowed His Spirit and His grace. The revelation of God in the burning bush is indeed an image of the revelation which God makes of Himself in Christ Jesus and in the gift of divine grace.

Father Marie-Eugene goes on to say that it is in grace itself that the living God reveals Himself and makes Himself known and experienced as self-giving love. It is in grace that each of the divine Persons reveals Himself: "As for the gaze of the contemplative, of the holy person who penetrates into God Himself thanks to this participation in divine life conferred by baptism: what does it discover? It discovers its connaturality, it discovers love. God is love. This gaze discovers the three divine Persons."[17] Only charity, which is the *science of love*, imparts full knowledge of God:

> In a certain measure we can experience the charity which is given to us, and since it is of the same nature as God, we can without illusion apply and transfer to God the notion we have of our own love, our supernatural charity.[18]

This is why Father Marie-Eugene considers that a desire for knowledge of God is an ordinary requirement in the life of any Christian who wants to grow in love of God and neighbor:

> The transcendence of God is a fact, and there is no question of our violating it. But we may gaze upon it, grasp something of it, and it pleases God to give us a certain experience of it, a certain understanding. Contemplation can and should tend to this knowledge of God in Himself. [...] We can and we should aspire to know Him through faith.[19]

Such is the knowledge of God, living and transforming, given to the simple gaze of faith and contemplation. It shows the soul *its sublime dignity and beauty* by revealing to it its grace and the splendor of the One who dwells within it. This is what makes the baptized person a witness of the living God. Father Marie-Eugene expresses his longing thus:

> May we ourselves say, in a certain sense, what our Lord said to Nicodemus: "No one goes to God of himself, only one bears witness to Him," and I, too, can bear witness. For although we have not been there, and are not like our Lord, in the unity of Persons, we can still invoke our experience of God sometimes, to affirm that it is possible and to give to others the taste and desire for it.[20]

Baptismal grace, "an anchor in life"

> In all of creation, God can give nothing more perfect than grace, the created participation in His nature. God therefore has no keener joy than that which He experiences in pouring out His grace.[21]

In constant references to the Second Letter of Peter and to Christian tradition which has commented upon it, Father Marie-Eugene will say of grace that *it is a participation in divine life.*[22] He sees in grace our greatest treasure, a supernatural gift bestowed on us in Christ, without which we could not turn toward God. All his teaching on prayer, our approach to God, our realization of union with God, and our resemblance to Christ Jesus which is the term and end of the spiritual life, is based on the doctrine of baptismal grace. The apostolate and the witness which should accompany it are effective only through the vitality of the grace which indwells and animates the baptized person. The dynamism of the Christian life is identified with the dynamism of grace.[23]

Because it is a *real* participation in divine life, grace imparts to us the very life of God. It *marks us* as with a seal, *for God and for Trinitarian life*.[24] In simple and convincing words Father Marie-Eugene recalls this function of baptismal grace, too often misunderstood and yet so essential:

> The Christian life is not only a moral life, it does not consist merely in avoiding this or that sin. It consists primarily in doing something positive. [...] Our vital Christian energies are grace, and sonship of God, and the consequent carrying out in this world of our role as His children. Our performance will be imperfect, but we carry on in faith and in reality. Our role as God's children consists in uniting ourselves to Him, and, with God the Father, breathing Love, as St.

> John of the Cross says, breathing the Holy Spirit.[25]

In this union with the divine life, grace effects in us a unique perfection, that of God. "There is only one perfection," Father Marie-Eugene said toward the end of his life. "It is that of the Father and the Son who love each other. It is substantial Love. Our love, though finite, is the same."[26]

Grace, which has as its goal the union of every person with God, cannot be limited by particular modalities. Understood in its filial dimension, it develops in us the true freedom of the children of God:

> Christian perfection is independent of all modalities, all human means, all natural perfections, whether sensory, intellectual, or even moral. Perfection for us, Christian perfection, consists in attaining to God. Our perfection is in God, it is union with God, and consequently it is the full development of our baptismal grace. It is nowhere else to be found, it is no other thing than this. All ways, methods, means, all forms of asceticism, should lead us to this.[27]

Freeing the supernatural life from the various natural or "mystical" modalities which may accompany it is an essential aspect of the teaching of Father

Marie-Eugene. It is a characteristic dimension of his theology. He saw the importance of this not only because it allows grace to flower freely in each person, but also because it prepares an opening for the Gospel message in all settings, regardless of emotional and cultural differences.

Regarding this problem of openness to the Gospel message and the teaching of supernatural realities, he wrote:

> It is a problem of humanism more than of grace. We are accustomed to present the supernatural in formulas and methods consonant with our Western and Mediterranean humanism. Only with difficulty do we imagine that it could reach souls except through these modalities, for our personal experience is limited to them. And yet the supernatural is independent and autonomous. Apart from revealed dogmatic formulas, which are necessary vehicles of divine truth, the rest can vary to a certain extent. God is free, independent of human modes. He has infinitely varied ways of communicating Himself, and chooses what is best adapted to each soul and each civilization.[28]

Father Marie-Eugene will again emphasize the fact that this union with God through grace cannot be effected without our consent and collaboration:

"God makes us free. He has given us free wills and He has a sovereign respect for our liberty. He will never sanctify us without our consent."[29] The spiritual life of a Christian cannot develop without the complete gift of self, rooted in Christ's self-giving and obedient to the action of the Holy Spirit.[30] Holiness will consist in this free and loving submission of our whole being to God:

> Basic to everything, to the collaboration which we establish with God on the contemplative level and to the spiritual life, there must be the recognition of God's transcendence and authority. There must be submission to God, and yet more, the gift of all we have and all we are.[31]

The gift of self will be all the more complete in that it will extend to our most spiritual and personal goods: our faculties of intellect and free will: "To hand over our intellect, our will, our very self, is the ultimate gift we can offer God. We have nothing better to give. This is what He looks for."[32]

Our gift must be as total as this because the life of grace extends to the whole person: "All our being, all our soul is involved in this approach to God." Grace is *grafted* upon human nature.[33] It is joined to the richness and complexity of our human person in order to orient us to God with all our powers:

> Human perfection, Christian perfection, is present in this journey toward the goal, toward God; it is present in the activity of the powers and energies at all levels as they move toward God. The whole person must arrive at the goal; no part is excluded.[34]

Not even the powers of the senses are left out. They will find their place within this synthesis of all love's capacities which are to be fulfilled by grace.

This kind of submission of the human person to the divine, through grace and the presence of the Holy Spirit, is ordinarily perceived as an impoverishment. Yet in truth it is the source of a genuine enrichment, a real flowering of the entire human person.[35] "Love humbles itself even though it is all powerful, in order to exalt those it loves," says Father Marie-Eugene.[36] Considering the example of the first disciples of Jesus and of the saints who have enhanced the history of the Church, he adds:

> Apostles, like Jesus Christ, are glorified by the Spirit of Love who possesses them. The human personality is elevated and broadened by this presence and possession of the Spirit. The senses are purified, the intellect refined, the will strengthened, and an integral human balance is established. A certain gift of wholeness comes into being through the mysterious influence of the divine presence.[37]

All Christians, from the moment of baptism, are called to know and participate in these riches of divine life and supernatural love which the grace of the sacrament contains in germ. And more — we should become the conscious collaborators of the sanctifying action of the Holy Spirit within us. We do this first of all by faith: "The supernatural world which is opened up to us in baptism is not a matter of refreshing water or fire which we can feel. It is a reality to which we adhere by faith."[38] This adherence to the supernatural world through faith strengthens hope and nourishes charity:

> Once we are aware of our baptismal grace, the seal it confers, the light it gives, the orientation it insures, and the hope it bestows, we have an anchor in life for our soul.[39]

The primacy which Father Marie-Eugene gives to grace in his teaching attests its importance for the entire Christian life. His insistence on speaking of it and describing its riches is a pressing invitation to us to consider it *more attentively, more often*:

> Our great treasure is our baptismal grace. We must value it rightly, above all else. It determines our eternal destiny and throws its light on the path we should follow in this world, the furrow we are meant to plough.[40]

In relating the highest realities of the life of union with God — contemplation, the union of the will with God, the contemplative discovery of the mystery of the Church, and transformation in Christ Jesus — to the ordinary development of baptismal grace, Father Marie-Eugene gives to his teaching the quality of universality which he finds in the masters of Carmel, and which he sees confirmed in the far-reaching radiance of the holiness of Thérèse of the Child Jesus.[41]

Prayer: union with God

In Jesus, we Christians bear the seal of our God. We belong to Him through our baptismal consecration, which makes of us other Christs. The dignity which grace confers upon us pervades our entire person, our whole being and every moment of our lives. We go to God with all we are and all we do. To direct our being and life to God, to submit them to Him so as to receive His grace, to grow in love and to be united to Him: this is the role which Christian prayer ought to fulfill: "What is prayer? Prayer is 'the lifting up of the soul to God.' Take away, if you will, the words 'lifting up.' Prayer is the movement of our whole self, our person, toward God. Prayer is making contact with God in order to converse with Him."[42]

Such an exchange implies union between the person and God. Only grace makes this possible. Grace is filial, its essential movement is to turn to God, to tend to Him as a child to its father. Prayer, *which identifies itself with every vital movement of grace in our soul*,[43] fulfills perfectly the character of a child of God. Thus Father Marie-Eugene will say of prayer that it is basically union with God: "Prayer is an exercise of union, a lifting of the soul to God, union with God."[44] There is no question here of proposing a new method of prayer. His teaching points to what is the foundation of every prayer, whether it be vocal or silent, personal, communal, or liturgical. The essence of prayer consists in the search for God through faith and love, in order to be united with Him and to remain in His presence.

Father Marie-Eugene draws the substance of his masterful exposition of prayer not only from the doctors of Carmel, whose teaching is confirmed by their lofty personal experience of prayer, but still more from his contemplation of the Christ he finds in the Gospels.

When he searches for Christ, he finds Him at prayer: "One truth stands out clearly when we study our Lord: He prayed much."[45]

He watches Christ praying at Nazareth. Jesus "spends almost thirty years in Nazareth, because He judges that the most important role He has to fulfill is that of an ordinary, hidden life, which will leave

Him free for the primary duty of prayer."[46] Prayer, then, will be the ordinary stance of Christians and will create the rhythm of our daily lives.

Father Marie-Eugene watches Jesus at prayer during His public life. "The evangelists are unanimous on this point. Throughout His entire life, Christ repeatedly retires into solitude to pray."[47] The services we have to perform, the public or private duties to be discharged, the most important tasks on our agenda, will require much prayer, an ever deepening union with God, and a renewed and ever more personal union with Christ Jesus.

In the night of Gethsemane, during the Passion, and on Calvary, Jesus' prayer for the salvation of mankind becomes agonized beneath the weight of the sin of the world.

> It is this prayer of suffering, this grief-filled prayer whose agony is caused by contradiction, of hell's assault on the heaven within Him, it is this prayer that is redemptive.[48]

The Church, united to Christ as His own body, prolongs within each Christian the redemptive prayer of Jesus in His Passion:

> Christ, now in heaven, dies no more, the apostle St. Paul tells us, but He has left to His Church the anguish resulting from the opposition between sin and divinity. He

> has left to Christians the responsibility of realizing the prayer of union; He has left to us also the role of continuing the agonized prayer of Gethsemane.[49]

Before the faith-filled gaze of Father Marie-Eugene, refined by contemplation, the prayer of Christ is rooted in the mystery of the hypostatic union.

Through the Incarnation the Word was made flesh. He became man, without ceasing to be eternally turned toward God, being God. Christ, through His humanity substantially united to the divinity and sanctified by the fulness of grace, understands the mystery dwelling within Him, contemplates God, and offers Himself to the sovereignty of the Word:

> In Christ, divinity penetrates humanity. Humanity itself is plunged into divinity by a very simple gaze, a gaze which is an intuitive knowledge of God [...] The union, then, is perfect: God's penetration into man, and at the same time man's penetration into God, humanity's penetration into God, by the very simple gaze of the intuitive vision.[50]

"The hypostatic union places our Lord in a state of continual prayer," Father Marie-Eugene tells us.[51] Through this prayer "Christ plunges into the intimate life of God in the Blessed Trinity" which His beatific vision reveals to Him. Such is the prayer of Christ, a prayer of union, "the perfect and experienced realization of the hypostatic union in Christ."[52]

These are the luminous mother lodes, the inexhaustible veins of the mystery of Christ, already described by St. John of the Cross in his *Spiritual Canticle*. Father Marie-Eugene tells us that they are revealed to the soul by means of a connatural knowledge which grace gives, together with the Christ from Whom it flows and to Whom it unites the soul.

In this light of Christ Jesus, Christian prayer, which becomes contemplative through the action of the Holy Spirit, "is led to its essential elements, simplified without being weakened, and thus placed within the reach of all souls."[53] From his wide spiritual and human experience, Father Marie-Eugene understood that in order that this teaching might be lived out by all people in their very diverse situations, it was necessary to emphasize what is most important in prayer and what makes it nourishing and desirable, namely, contact with God through faith and in love. "We should therefore be convinced about what the essence of prayer truly is. It is making contact with God in order to be enriched by Him, to establish communication with Him through faith, by an act of love."[54] Rendered contemplative through the gifts of the Holy Spirit, prayer is, then, union with God, "an exchange, a descent of God into the soul."[55] In regard to methods of prayer and ways of becoming recollected, Father Marie-Eugene, without in any way downgrading them, recommends freedom and flexibility: "We each find our own way of making contact with God and maintaining it."[56]

Let us consider the witness of Marie Pila:

> Father therefore proposed a wholly simple prayer, disengaged not only from all that could be extraordinary, but even from the experiential and the savored. He proposed a prayer of faith, in which one should keep one's gaze fixed on God; a prayer which is nothing else than "a simple gaze at God" stripped of all else; a prayer which leads to the heights even as it led St. Thérèse of the Child Jesus herself.[57]

Response to the expectations of the world

For us Christians, the grandeur of our vocation is not achieved simply by the salvation of our own souls, nor by our turning away from this world in which we live and the times in which it is given to us to play a part. Resemblance to Christ Jesus "does not isolate persons from the world by leading them to God. It associates them with the intense life of the Church in this world."[58]

Father Marie-Eugene often allows us to see the loving and at times sorrowing attention he turns to the humanity of his day, which is also our day, and to the Church as well. He witnessed the triumphant domination of communism and its negative power over all that is at the foundation of man's worship of God: freedom and grace.[59] In his day there were, too, the sometimes anxious questionings of the Church as to how best to assure her presence in the world and her apostolate.[60]

Father Marie-Eugene's answers reveal the strength of his faith in the Holy Spirit as the prime mover in all action that can be called Christian. They are also the result of his personal experience of an apostolate whose growth he longed to see, and the ongoing manifestation of its power and fruitfulness.[61]

What is asked of a witness?

> We look for the kind of spiritual radiance which comes from the soul, which we can glimpse sometimes on a person's face, which shines out in our attitudes, uprightness, in a whole life.[62]

How will we be present to the world and witness to it?

> But the main witness we ought to give is the witness *of what we are*. It is the witness of the Christian life, of the life of Christ which we

> bear within us. It is the witness of the Holy Spirit who is our Guest.[63]
>
> What will be the first task of the witness?
>
> Our first duty will not necessarily be to act. We must act, yes, but our first duty will be to act *well*, to develop our grace and union with Christ, so that our action may be truly good, truly apostolic, in other words, intimate collaboration.[64]

This means that apostles should strive for holiness, perfect union with God.

The life of grace reaches its fulness and fruitful radiance in the presence of the Holy Spirit: "The Spirit is our Guest, a living flame in us, a light. He is our friend. He is truly in us, He sanctifies us and divinizes us constantly."[65] The Holy Spirit's presence in a soul is living and active. Only living faith, purified by love, perceives this:

> It is not a matter of believing in the Holy Spirit in a vague sort of way. We must believe in Him as a living reality, a living, intelligent, all-powerful Person, a Person who knows what He *wants*, who does what He *wills*, and who knows where He is going.[66]

With St. Paul, Father Marie-Eugene recognizes in this presence of the Holy Spirit the characteristic mark of the Christian: "All who are led by the Spirit of God are sons of God."[67]

Father Marie-Eugene draws but one conclusion from this, but it is essential to the radiance of apostles and the fruitfulness of their activity:

> Christians, consequently — and not only those who have offices and responsibilities but all Christians — ought to live in contact with the Holy Spirit.[68]

Union with God is the foundation of the apostolate, for it is ordered to fruitfulness, to the development of the Church:

> The Kingdom of God is the whole Christ, the Church. This Kingdom is therefore primarily spiritual, since it is constituted by Christ and by the life of grace which He pours into our souls. It is spiritual because the Holy Spirit animates it. He is its soul.[69]

Union with God is truly "the collaboration which we owe to the Holy Spirit"[70] in the upbuilding of the Kingdom of God, for in order to be apostles, perfect workers in the Kingdom, "we must already be possessed by the Holy Spirit."[71]

Here we return to one of the most basic aspects of the Christian life, the indissoluble union between Christian contemplation and action. The union is indissoluble because it is rooted in the very nature of grace, which, in divinizing us, unites us to God, and in becoming incarnate, makes us bear the weight of the sin of mankind.

When it is perfect, this union has another name, that of sanctity: "Christian perfection and contemplative perfection consist in this union and this realization of Christ Jesus our Lord."[72] It associates Christians with the entire life of Christ. It harmonizes all the movements of their souls with the soul of Christ and reveals to them the expectations of their times:

> They pray with Christ, in the light which is given. And this light is not just a general light regarding the divine presence in their souls. Given at its own moment, this light reveals both the eternal Church and the Church in time.[73]

Sanctity is the united response of a person and God, made to the expectations and hopes of each era, each generation. "The saint," writes Father Marie-Eugene in *I Want to See God*, "belongs to a particular period, race or nation, a very definite stage in the full development of the mystical Body of Christ. The divine and eternal elements within sanctity do not hinder, rather they oblige it to be incarnated in the most human elements of an era."[74] But sanctity is above all the response of God's mercy to the greatest suffering of humanity: sin.

The humanity of our times, "wounded and stripped"

> The more the saints are possessed by love, the closer they are to us, for in divinizing them charity causes them to enter into the depths of sin, which is the great affliction of mankind.[75]

Father Marie-Eugene believed that contemporary mankind's greatest affliction lies in its practical ignorance of God, its indifference to its own influence on the world and souls, and its lack of a theological life: "the great misery is lack of faith."[76]

He saw the humanity of our times as wounded and stripped of its noblest values, like the man attacked by robbers on the road to Jericho.[77] "In this man fallen by the wayside, wounded and stripped by robbers and left half dead, I see the humanity of our times."[78]

Wounded by sin, ignorant of supernatural realities and the power of forgiveness, humanity can no longer help itself. It has lost the use of the life of grace:

> The humanity of our times seems to me like this poor man... it has been robbed by the devil and can no longer walk or turn toward God. People laid low by the devil's blows, and unable to return to God, these are the

> ones who should arouse our deepest compassion. This man by the roadside is truly the symbol Jesus gives us for the humanity of our times.[79]

This misery moved Father Marie-Eugene, because it is deeper and more serious than any material misery. And because it touches the inner realities of the spirit, he longed to relieve it with the love and mercy of God:

> God so loved the world, He so pitied its sin, that He sent His only Son. And the Son had such pity for this sin of man's, this absence of God from souls and their powerlessness to reach God because of their sin, that He delivered Himself up, He mounted the Cross.[80]

This movement toward sinners, to relieve their misery, is the movement of divine Love, which wrought the Incarnation, the Redemption, and the Church. It is the movement of *the perfect apostolate, because it is one with the deeds and actions of Jesus*.[81] It is the movement of charity:

> The charity of Christians should embrace the whole world and especially the most unfortunate. Our charity ought to resemble that of God, which becomes mercy when it encounters poverty and misery. The char-

> ity of Christians should do the same; it shares God's nature. Flowing from God, it should be transformed into mercy.[82]

The duty of Christians, of apostles, is therefore to bear witness today as always to the source of their life, the divine flame which dwells within and animates them, and to this end, to deliver themselves over to the grace of God:

> This is the meaning of our life: to seek God, to find Him, to make contact with Him, and to give Him to others. To set people on our donkey, to bandage their wounds, to guide them by means of our prayer, to sacrifice ourselves entirely in order to lead them to God.... They suffer physical hunger and thirst. We have given them food and drink.... Their hunger and thirst are spiritual. We have given them God.[83]

Rev. Charles Niqueux
Centre Notre-Dame de Vie
May 8, 1990

Notes

[1] Rev. Marie-Eugene, Conference of May 18, 1958, published in the French periodical, *Carmel*, 1988, 3-4, n. 51, 342.

[2] "My vocation is theological, I was made to lead souls to God, to divine union." These words of Father Marie-Eugene, reported by Marie Pila, describe his vocation, *God's plan for him*. They also characterize his teaching, manifesting the grace given him and the fruit of his mission in the Church. (Cf. M. Pila, *"Le Fondateur"* ["The Founder"], in *Carmel*, special issue, *"Le Père Marie-Eugène de l'Enfant Jésus"* ["Father Marie-Eugene of the Child Jesus"], March 1968, 112-128; text reprinted in *Carmel*, 1988/3-4, n. 51, 233-249).

[3] Cf. "Baptismal Grace," 29.

[4] *Ibid.*, 45.

[5] *Ibid.*, 38.

[6] Such a perspective might seem very far from current human aspirations, had it not just been recalled to us as essential to the renewal of evangelization to which Pope John Paul II invites all Christians in his Apostolic Exhortation on the Laity (*Christifideles laici,* December 30, 1988).

In similar words, John Paul II considers the dignity of man in the light of God: "The dignity of the person is manifested in all its radiance when the person's origin and destiny are considered: created by God in His image and likeness as well as redeemed by the most precious blood of Christ, the person is called to be a 'child in the Son' and a living temple of the Spirit, destined for the eternal life of blessed communion with God" (*Christifideles laici*, n. 37).

The Apostolic Exhortation develops in its first chapter the necessity for all Christians to follow the way of holiness in order to realize this evangelical renewal. Many topics introduced by Father Marie-Eugene could illustrate this objective. Citing the Apostolic Exhortation in this introduction is therefore an invitation to us to turn to it frequently, as well as to the conciliar texts it evokes, particularly those concerning the universal call to holiness.

[7] Father Marie-Eugene, *I Want to See God: A Practical Synthesis of Carmelite Spirituality*, 2 vols. tr. by Sr. M. Verna Clare, C.S.C. (Fides Publishers, 1955; Christian Classics, 1997), vol. 1, 42. Father Marie-Eugene thus reiterates the Christian tradition

which has always affirmed the noble destiny of man manifested in Christ (cf. *Christifideles laici*, n. 17).

[8] *Christifideles laici*, n. 16.

[9] Father Marie-Eugene thus explains this right: "Consequently each of us, assuming that we have a function, has a strict right to grace, to the action and assistance of the Holy Spirit in fulfilling perfectly the function entrusted to us by our grace" ("The Perfect Apostle," 278).

[10] Cf. *Christifideles laici*, n. 17.

[11] "The Activity of God in Prayer," 88.

[12] "The Mystery of God," 9.

[13] Conference of August 18, 1966 (unpublished).

[14] Cf. Conference of August 18, 1957 (unpublished): "God is love, He acts through love, He gives love. This definition, 'God is love,' leads us more deeply into God than all others, such as: God is Spirit — God is transcendent Being — God is self-subsistent Being — because this definition leads us into the intimate life of God."

[15] "The Mystery of God," 12.

[16] *Ibid.*, 16.

[17] Conference of August 18, 1957.

[18] Conference of August 18, 1966. To explain this life which is in God and perhaps still more to obtain the adherence of faith to the supernatural realities he is speaking of, Father Marie-Eugene stresses the inadequacy of concepts and prefers images and symbols which express movement:

"We use separate notions, concepts. How can we speak or explain anything without choosing images for the imagination and concepts for the intellect? Obviously the images of the burning bush, of the ocean moving back and forth with the tides seem to us much more powerful and exact than the concept, which in itself seems poor by comparison since it can only be contained within the measure of our intellect" (*ibid.*).

On the subject of expressing supernatural realities, he writes in *I Want to See God*:

> "This expression will abandon the language of concepts, too precise to convey the wealth of richness of the realities under consideration and the reactions produced throughout the entire human person. It will turn naturally to images, symbols, words with undefined meanings, which are vaster, less restricted, and therefore better adapted to the infinite:

and mystical experience will charge this lyricism with the warmth and powerful savor of the impression received" (vol. 1, 502-504).

[19] "The Mystery of God," 17, 19.

[20] *Ibid.*, 27.

[21] *I Want to See God*, vol. 1, 30.

[22] Cf. 2 Peter 1:4. It is a question of created grace, whereby uncreated grace, that is, the Holy Spirit Himself, dwells within us.

[23] Father Marie-Eugene's teaching on grace is highly developed. It would be helpful to consult the pages in *I Want to See God* which treat of it (cf. "Baptismal Grace," note 9). The lines which follow are simply intended to bring out certain aspects stressing the theological dimension of this teaching which can be applied to every Christian life: union with God through grace; the distinction between supernatural modalities; the involvement of every human life in grace.

[24] Cf. "Baptismal Grace," 37.

[25] "Great Christian Truths," 160.

[26] R. Regue, *Père Marie Eugène de l'Enfant-Jésus, maître spirituel pour notre temps* [*Father Marie-Eugene of the Child Jesus, Spiritual Master for Our Times*], (Éditions du Carmel, 1978), 122.

[27] "Baptismal Grace," 40.

[28] Father Marie-Eugene, *Père d'une multitude — Lettres autobiographiques* [*Father of a Multitude — Autobiographical Letters*], (Fayard, 1988), 162.

[29] Father Marie-Eugene, *"Le don de soi"* ["The gift of self"] Conference of August 2, 1961, published in *Carmel*, 1988/3-4, n. 51, 328.

[30] Cf. *I Want to See God*, vol. 1, 368: "The fundamental disposition of Christ, the total gift of self, is a basically Christian disposition. It identifies one with Christ in one's depths, and without it all imitation of Jesus can only be superficial and perhaps vain external formalism. To belong to Christ one must be handed over to Him as He is to God, for we are Christ's and Christ is God's."

[31] *"Le don de soi,"* 329.

[32] *Ibid.*, 330.

[33] Cf. *I Want to See God*, vol.1, 26: "Grafted upon human nature with its living organism of infused virtues and gifts of the Holy

Spirit, grace espouses perfectly the forms of the human complex and takes hold of all its powers and activities. Invading it, it progressively penetrates and dominates the human faculties, while freeing them from their egotistic and disordered tendencies. Filial, it draws them, after having conquered them, in its movement toward this interior God, Father of light and mercy, and offers them to Him now purified and faithful, wholly subject to His lights and His action."

[34] "Baptismal Grace," 43-44.

[35] There is not the least contradiction in the Christian life; regarding the *apparent oppositions* accompanying the life of grace, which take their rise from the mystery of Christ Himself, Father Marie-Eugene writes:

"These contradictions or apparent oppositions fall under the law of divine love which contains them within itself as a part of its richness, and marks its works with them as with a personal signature. This love is incarnate and divine, it diffuses joy and tribulation, it produces a light which is darkness. Christ Jesus, who assures its reign here below, is the Word made flesh. Without ceasing to enjoy the beatific vision, He experienced the deepest suffering possible in this world, and triumphed in the end by dying on the cross" (*I Want to See God*, vol. 2, 616-617). Cf. also F.-M. Lethel, *"Dans le Christ Jésus"* ["In Christ Jesus"], *Carmel*, 1988/3-4, n. 51, p. 271.

[36] *I Want to See God*, vol. 2, 663.

[37] *Ibid.*

[38] "Daily Prayer," 123.

[39] "Baptismal Grace," 46.

[40] *Ibid.*, 45.

[41] Cf. Father Marie-Eugene, *Under the Torrent of His Love*, Alba House, 1995, 146:

"At the threshold of this new world of ours, greater and more powerful than preceding ones because it has embraced and conquered the universe, more tormented also and more divided, God has placed Thérèse of the Child Jesus, to reveal Love and make Love loved, to organize an immense legion of little souls who have experienced Love and are capable of waging its difficult battles here below.

"It is always risky to prophesy. But I do not call it prophesying; rather it is simply an expression of my thought and conviction — based on the work already accomplished, the vastness of the field in which she exerts her influence, which is the entire world, and the power and purity of the light she casts about her — when I affirm that Thérèse will be, in fact already is, one of the great spiritual teachers of the Church, one of the most proficient spiritual guides of all times." (See the original French title, *Ton amour a grandi avec moi. Un génie spirituel, Thérèse de Lisieux*, Éditions du Carmel, Venasque, 1987, pp. 168-169.)

42 "Prayer as Contact with God," 53. This last expression will recall the essence of St. Teresa of Avila's definition of prayer, namely "a simple exchange of friendship in which one often converses alone with God, knowing that one is loved by Him" (*ibid.*, n. 3).

43 *I Want to See God*, vol. 1, 52.

44 "The Perfect Contemplative Prayer of Christ," 151.

45 *Ibid.*, 142.

46 *Ibid.*, 143-144.

47 *Ibid.*, 144.

48 *Ibid.*, 157.

49 *Ibid.*, 157.

50 *Ibid.*, 145.

51 Quoted by F.-M. Lethel, *"Dans le Christ Jésus,"* 275.

52 "The Perfect Contemplative Prayer of Christ," 147.

53 Cf. Marie Pila, *"Le Fondateur,"* 121. The essential elements of prayer, which are the act of faith and the action of the Holy Spirit through the gifts, are detailed in "Prayer as Contact with God" and "The Activity of God in Prayer."

54 "Daily Prayer," 115.

55 "The Activity of God in Prayer," 87.

56 "Daily Prayer," 114.

57 Marie Pila, "*Le Fondateur*," 121.

58 *I Want to See God*, vol. 2, 614.

59 Cf. *"Le don de soi,"* n. 51, 329: "God wants the homage of our freedom. He has made us free, because He wants this homage of our freedom."

60 Cf. R. Regue, *"Croire en l'Esprit Saint — L'expérience du Père Marie-Eugène de l'E.J."*["To believe in the Holy Spirit — The experience of Father Marie-Eugene"], in *Viens Esprit Saint* [*Come Holy Spirit*], Éditions du Carmel, 1988, 268.

61 Cf. Marie Pila, *"Le Fondateur,"* 125: "Father Marie-Eugene was

made for action, he was a planner, he loved enterprise and challenge, but his love of action stemmed from his love for the Church and souls, and this love was immense. [...] His apostle's soul burned with a consuming zeal. Sensing the limits placed on this zeal by his being a religious, he said to his sons and daughters of Notre-Dame de Vie: 'You will go where I cannot go.' And we recall his joy at the first departure for distant lands: 'How happy it makes me to see you scattering! You have not been chosen to stay on the sidelines, to watch and pray, but to be thrown into the crowd, to mix with the throngs like leaven, and to produce its action as long as it is capable of acting'."

62 "Presence and Witness," 234.

63 *Ibid.*, 233.

64 "The Perfect Apostle," 279.

65 "The Mystery of God," 24.

66 "The Primacy of the Holy Spirit," 201.

67 Rm 8:14.

68 "The Primacy of the Holy Spirit," 201.

69 "Building the Kingdom," 177.

70 "The Primacy of the Holy Spirit," 210.

71 "Presence and Witness," 238.

72 *I Want to See God*, vol. 2, 605.

73 "The Perfect Apostle," 284.

74 *I Want to See God*, vol. 2, 617.

75 *Ibid.*, vol. 2, 614.

76 Conference of August 22, 1959 (unpublished).

77 Cf. Lk 10:29-37.

78 Conference of August 22, 1959.

79 *Ibid.*

80 *Ibid.*

81 *I Want to See God*, vol. 2, 622.

82 Conference of August 22, 1959.

83 *Ibid.*

The teaching given here by Father Marie-Eugene was addressed to a very wide audience.

The first two texts, included in Part One, are conferences given in 1962:

Part One — Foundations:
"The Mystery of God," Notre-Dame de Vie
(September 3, 1962).
"Baptismal Grace," Marseille (February 23, 1962).

Part Two and Part Three are compiled from two series of public conferences, forming a continuous teaching:

Part Two — Toward a Transformation of Love:
Conferences at Carpentras
(May 2, 9 and 16; June 13, 1957).

Part Three — Possessed by the Spirit:
Conferences at Marseille
(February 1, 4, 8, 11 and 15, 1956).

In every case the written text was finalized at the time of taping. The oral style has been preserved, with Father Marie-Eugene's own direct, vigorous manner of presentation. Titles and notes have been added for the present edition.

Most frequent references are to the following editions of the Masters of Carmel:

St. Teresa of Avila: *Complete Works*
St. John of the Cross: *Spiritual Works*
St. Thérèse of the Child Jesus: *Autobiographical Manuscripts, Last Conversations, A Memoir of My Sister, St. Thérèse*
Marie-Eugene of the Child Jesus: *I Want to See God*

Biblical references are taken from the Revised Standard Version

Part One — Foundations

The Mystery of God

I would like to describe and explain the theological foundations of the road which leads to contemplation. In the past such a plan might have seemed pretentious. Today, on the contrary, I believe this teaching should be opened up to the whole world.

To look at God

The contemplation to which I would like to lead you, and which I consider as our goal, is not contemplation accompanied by mystical graces. If God wishes to give these to you, He will do so, but this is not what we are directly aiming at. According to St. Thomas' definition, contemplation is in plain language a simple gaze on Truth, that is, on God.[1] After giving this definition, St. Thomas tells us that the chief object of contemplation is *God*.[2] There are many secondary objects, but the chief one is God. Do not be surprised, therefore, that in this first conference we shall try to fix our gaze upon God, our end.

What is God? God is the object of contemplation, the final end to which we tend. This is why I would like to speak to you of God.

At the source of mission

My second reason is that knowledge of God and lights about Him — we see this in the lives of the saints and also in the teaching of St. John of the Cross — are extremely fruitful in transforming the soul, and above all the soul of the apostle. The lives of the great saints, those especially who had important missions, such as Moses, St. Paul, St. Ignatius, St. John of the Cross, or St. Teresa, are marked in the beginning by some great light about God, by what St. John of the Cross calls "a substantial touch"[3] or a light about God Himself.

For Moses as for St. Paul, this light about God, which is not a new revelation but a deeper knowledge of God, is the source of their missions. It is the principle of a transformation, a change, and will enlighten them all along their journey.

We are familiar enough with St. Paul to know that the vision he had on the road to Damascus not only transformed him, sinner that he was, into a Christian and an apostle. In this vision he found absolutely everything: his mission as an apostle and the light which he described later on. His time in prison gave him the opportunity to explain the graces he had received. His contemplative letters are but an unfolding of this vision which he had on the road to Damascus.

And for us, who are just beginning our journey to God, what should we do? Look at God, try to gaze at God.

I — GOD IS INFINITE, AND EVER MOVING

What is God?

The transcendent God

God is infinite Being, the only Being who subsists in Himself, who has neither cause nor source, who always was and always will be. He is the only infinite being, above all, transcendent, inaccessible in Himself, and the principle of everything else. We ought to defend this transcendence of God. The Church does. She has shown us how firmly she holds to it. She considers it essential, even though many souls shy away from it.

God is, then, the infinite, transcendent Being, He who is: "I am who I am."[4] He is infinite in His eternity: beyond time therefore, for He is outside of time. He is infinite in His perfections, in His dimensions, in everything. God is the infinite Being in whom we can find no increase. There is no development in God, since any increase or growth in perfection would imply that He had not been perfect from the beginning.

Connected with this infinity there is — from our human point of view — a certain stability: *"Tu autem idem ipse es et anni tui non deficient"* ("But you are the same, and your years have no end").[5] The psalmist emphasizes this stability of God, this absence of change. We change our clothes; nature too changes its appearance. God does not change — *"Tu autem idem ipse es"* — because He is infinite.

God is wrapped in shadows

The gaze of our simple reason, disconcerted by the inaccessible transcendence of God, can see nothing but darkness. The psalmist and other Old Testament writers understood this clearly: to our eyes God is wrapped in the shadow of His infinity because our intelligence is not adapted to infinity. We are blinded by God, just as we are blinded by the brilliance of the noonday sun. For this reason, we say that God is darkness, God is wrapped in shadows.

Yet there are saints to whom God has revealed something of what lies in the shadows. St. John is an example. In the prologue of his Gospel he says: "In the beginning was the Word, and the Word was with God, and the Word was God." And he adds, "And in Him was life."[6] There is no immobility in this infinity. It is we who create the immobility, in a sense, through our powerlessness to perceive the infinite. We ascribe immobility to God because for us, whatever does not develop or grow is immobile. No, in God both qualities exist. We will discover here antinomies, apparent contradictions. "In Him was life." There is life, movement.

Moses' vision: the burning bush

It seems to me that it was Moses who first revealed this to us, this life and movement, this apparent contradiction, this association of the movement and life in God with His infinity.

To Moses the concept of God's infinity was a familiar one. Some people have said justly that the desert is monotheistic, by reason of its infinitude, its silence. Its immensity reveals at least in some sense the infinity of God. The desert is monotheistic because it excludes lesser gods and confronts us with the immensity of God, the inaccessible God. Moses, educated in the court of Pharaoh and in the universities of Egypt, and having therefore received the highest culture of his day, left for the desert to shepherd the flocks of Jethro, his father-in-law. Growing accustomed to the infinitude of the desert, he formed in the silence and bareness of Sinai what we might call an impression of the immensity and transcendence of God.

We can observe, as a matter of fact, that shepherds and desert races are monotheistic. We know how Psichari[7] and others discovered the infinitude of God in the desert.

One day Moses sees something, a phenomenon, a bush which burns and is not consumed, a flame.[8] He certainly is used to seeing bushes burn. Down there in the desert of Sinai, it is the same as in our mountains. At a certain season shepherds burn the bushes, so that with the springtime fresh grass will grow up for their flocks. So there is nothing surprising about seeing the fire. What astonishes Moses is that the fire is not consuming the bush, which has perhaps been burning for days.

He says: "I must go over and see this fire that does not consume the bush," and he draws near to it. And we all know the welcome that he gets: "Stop! The ground where you are standing is holy." He takes off his shoes and draws closer. The voice is coming out of the fire. "Who are you, who speak to me?" "I am He who is, I am the God of Abraham, of Isaac, of your fathers." Reread this magnificent scene in Exodus. The voice rises: "I am He who is." And Moses knows Him, "He who is," the infinite, inaccessible, transcendent One. He knows Him well.

But what puzzles him is that this transcendent One is in motion. What is this fire, really? It is a symbolic vision, a theophany of God. God is not only inaccessible, transcendent. In addition to this, He is not obscure. No! God is light, and yet more, God is flame, a flame which leaps up, a blazing fire. God is a fire, shooting out sparks, sending forth rays. There He is!

This concept of God, a God obviously revealed in a symbol, enlightens Moses and transforms him. Precisely here we have an example of knowledge which penetrates the depths of the soul and which, as St. John of the Cross tells us, transforms it, marking it with a seal.[9] Henceforth, Moses, transformed by this light which is also heat, can act only under its influence. He will receive his mission to go to Egypt later, but here and now he is being prepared to carry it out by this symbolic vision. He will be able to hold his own against Pharaoh. He knows what God is like, this God who is inaccessible, infinite, this God who is flame and furnace. God is a consuming furnace, a consuming fire. This is what He is!

This is Moses' knowledge. And he enlightens us. He is charged to transmit to us the revelation he has been given.

The revelation of Jesus: God is a movement of Love

This revelation will be more fully developed in the Old Testament, but above all by our Lord in the New.

Our Lord enters Jerusalem, the intellectual and spiritual center of Palestine, of this people to whom He has come to announce the Good News. What is He going to do here? He will tell it to Nicodemus.[10] He will find an intelligent man, one of the Doctors of the Law, whom we are used to scorning a little because they were Pharisees and we see them commenting on the Torah. Among them there is, however, an intelligent man whom our Lord has chosen.

This Nicodemus, Doctor of the Law, a reserved man, comes by night. He has seen our Lord; and declares that He is from God. It is unfortunate for Jesus that He comes from Nazareth, from Galilee. If He had lived in Jerusalem, what a magnificent teacher of the law He would have made! But Nicodemus recognizes the hand of God: "Yes, Master, Rabbi, only one who comes from God could do the things you do."

Our Lord responds to the longing of this man, this great spirit, this soul of good will. He is going to speak with him about where He comes from. Where does He come from? He comes from the regions of

God. No one has been up there to this infinite realm. It has been seen in symbolic visions, like that of Moses in the desert perhaps. But no one has ever come forth from this blazing fire before, this infinitude, this transcendent Being that is God, to tell men about Him. One only has come down: "It is I." This is what our Lord says: the Son of Man alone comes from the regions of God, those transcendent regions. He alone can bear witness to them because He has seen them, experienced them.

St. John too will tell us[11] that he has seen and handled the Christ, not only in His humanity but, we might say, also in His divinity. John has touched Him in a sense, and will bear witness in his Gospel to the humanity of Christ, His actions, gestures, words, and at the same time to the transcendence of His divinity.

But here it is Jesus Himself speaking, and what does He tell us? He is going to tell us something about God, give us a kind of description. What will He teach us about this infinitude from which He comes? He says: in this infinitude, there is the Father. And He reveals an episode, a movement, as it were, of the Father. What is it? It is a movement, yes: "God so loved the world that He sent His Son."[12]

This is the fundamental, the essential deed which shows us the nature of God. Yes, this God is not only the blazing fire shooting out sparks and rays; the sparks arising from the fire are the angels, finite beings. God, one day, by this movement of love within Him, has done an action so powerful that He has emitted, so to speak, something of Himself: His Word, His Son.

Through this episode, we learn about God. God the Father, source of light, source of mercy, is a God of love. This movement that Moses grasped, this fire, is a fire of love.

An exchange of love within God

Through the witness given us about this movement of God, we can know God better. God is love, God is a blazing fire, a leaping flame. That is what God is.

The Father, source of love

God the Father, origin of all things, source of light and mercy, this "depth" of God we might say, this base, this hearth whence everything emanates, is love. Love diffuses goodness. God is good, God is love, and this love in Him creates a movement. God is infinite, but since He is love He is a force, a power of expansion.

Why this movement? This movement proceeds from love. Love is goodness which gives itself, which expands. Such movement is natural to it, it springs from its nature. This is what God is: the power of expansion. *Bonum diffusivum sui* (The Good is diffusive of itself). With our minds enlightened by faith, we can try to reason about this.

The Son, a luminous sheet of flame leaping upward

God is a hearth, God is a blazing fire, God is the power of expansion. What arises out of this infinite power of expansion? For the fact that God is movement — and we can grasp this in a sense — that He has revealed something of Himself to us, does not mean that we can set limits to Him. He remains infinite. This power of expansion that is God, this love which rises, this blaze, this force is always merging and expanding.

What is it that mounts on high? It is a luminous sheet of flame which rises from the infinite One, from God the Source, who is Father because He is Source. And this flame, this luminous sheet which rises up as a blanket of fog may rise up and cover the sea, or as a flash of light may leap up from a hearth: this is the Son. The Son is God engendered by God, for this sheet of flame is clearly equal to its source. God works within Himself, engenders within Himself: "In the beginning was the Word, and He was in God, and had life in Him." The Word who mounts up in this way from God bears "the stamp of His nature."[13] He is equal to the Father. This much we can say about Him.

At a given moment He will be ejected, as it were, projected in our human nature, to take possession of it, to come among us and become the Word incarnate. But always there has been this mounting, this sheet of light, this flame arising from the Infinite.

The Spirit, Love personified

The two Persons have but one occupation. Both are God, yet clearly there is only one God. How can this be? It is a mystery... the mystery of the intimate life of God, of the Trinity. To be able to speak about it is not the same as explaining it. But the divine Persons are endowed with intelligence. They can understand each other, look at each other and love each other.

They look at each other, and when the Father sees this luminous sheet of flame mounting from Himself, He cannot but admire it because He finds Himself in it. It still remains Himself in nature. And this God, who after creation found each of the beings He had brought into existence good,[14] who loved His work — how should He not love His Word who leaps forth from Him? God the Father loves His Word. The Word also has intelligence, and gazes at His Father. He looks at the Source whence He springs unceasingly, he sees the Father who engenders Him unceasingly as a furnace continually engenders flame and light. And He loves this Source. He finds Himself in it.

This is contemplation: the simple gaze of God upon His Word, of the Word upon His Father. From this contemplation is born mutual wonder and love of the divine nature, the love of two Persons. We know what is produced by this act of love of Father and Son. It is an act of infinite Love, substantial Love, the third Person of the Blessed Trinity. The two Persons are forever united in this common love, in this common breathing forth of the one Love which flows between them and fills them with joy.

Infinite joy

This expansive power which is God finds all its joy in engendering, in producing.... Only an infinite act, only an infinite fruit can satisfy Him, since He is infinite. The generation of the Word gives the Father infinite joy. The procession of the Holy Spirit gives the two Persons, Father and Son, infinite joy.

This movement does not take place in time, at a given moment. It has always been. God has always been like this; He is without beginning. The generation of the Word had no beginning, the procession of the Holy Spirit had no beginning, the happiness of God is without beginning. This is how it has always been. We must believe it. He has always been, and His happiness is infinite, in the measure of His "work." It is infinite because "the work" is infinite, because His generation and this procession are also infinite. They have no limits, they will never end. God will always engender, the Son will always spring forth, the spiration of love will flow between Father and Son unceasingly, forever and ever and ever.... And God is always happy, God is infinitely happy. There we have it, the happiness of God!

How good it is for us to cast a glance now and then at this happiness of God! Peaceful joy, triumphant joy, happiness inexhaustible, joy serene.... There is no storm here. The generation, the spiration produce no tempest, they are effects of the plenitude of God, they are not beyond His powers. There is no need of force, or any sort of explosion, to spirate the Holy Spirit. No, it is normal, it flows forth.

This is the happiness of God, an infinite happiness, which we ought to think about and try to contrast sometimes with all our changeableness, all the upheavals of our world, all the waves of pessimism we feel in face of the misfortunes which threaten us or which have already come upon us. To be able to say, "God is happy!" This ocean, this infinite fire that is God, is something we can contemplate. We are destined to return to Him. He is our fatherland.

To contemplate the Trinitarian mystery

I have offered you something about God, expressed haltingly perhaps, but it can be the object of our contemplation. Let us not be frightened by this Trinitarian mystery which is said to be inaccessible. True, it would certainly be pride to want to understand and explain it; it would be foolish. The transcendence of God is a fact and there is no question of our violating it. But we may gaze upon it, grasp something of it, and it pleases God to give us a certain experience of it, a certain understanding.

Contemplation can and should tend to this understanding of God in Himself. St. Teresa and St. John of the Cross tell us quite simply that at the summit of the spiritual life, of the path they trace out for us, is the knowledge of God, which St. Teresa does not hesitate to call "the intellectual vision of the Blessed Trinity."[15] It is not "a vision." It is a kind of understanding gained through connaturality, always through faith, but it is still understanding.

Thus it was told of St. Teresa that she understood the definition of the dogma of the Trinity in the catechism, and could see how it was. She grasped to a certain extent the distinction of Persons in God and how these three Persons are, so to say, in a nucleus, a center, a fire, a blaze. The same is true of St. John of the Cross. These two saints apprehended the Trinitarian mystery in different ways, the one through one Person, the other through another Person. St. Thérèse of the Child Jesus, too, was enthralled, fascinated by the mystery of the Trinity.

Allow me to say a few words about this. When St. Thérèse spoke of the Trinitarian mystery people said, "What is this! A child talking about the mystery of the Trinity — it is impossible!" Therefore aren't they implying that in her discovery of the mystery of the Trinity, in her descriptions, two Persons are left out? "Just think! For her to discover the Child Jesus is fine, for her to discover the Blessed Virgin.... But for her to discover the divine Persons!"

Clearly, people who thought this way were paying homage to the prejudices of our era, which hold that the mystery of the Trinity is far too lofty for us.... But let us depart from such judgments and prejudices, and let us not hesitate to yearn for the Trinity. We too have been told that we should not aspire to lofty perceptions. We do not aspire to the accidentals of the supernatural world, to mystical graces properly so called, which affect the senses. But we do desire knowledge of God, and we may ask for it.

What will we be doing in heaven if not finding God? We are not going there just to look up our cousins and nephews. We are going there to find God, to contemplate this inaccessible, infinite One and to grasp Him with the means, the instrument, the light of glory — the *lumen gloriae*[16] that shall be given us according to our charity. We will not relinquish this truth. Let us know how to affirm our teaching on it, clarifying our concepts and refusing to be content with vague slogans which often contain much error.

We may aspire to knowledge of God even in this world in a certain way, even through mystical graces if God so wills. If God were giving you Moses' vision in the desert, I would quite simply congratulate you. It would not be a misfortune, any more than if you received St. Paul's vision on the road to Damascus! These could be received without our losing our minds and being immediately consigned to a psychiatric hospital. Even if we were shaken up, like St. Paul, for some time, we would still have the advantage of all these riches, riches precious in the extreme.

In any case, though it is true that we should not aspire to mystical graces and their accidental embellishments, and to extraordinary ways of knowing God, and that it would be dangerous for us to do so, we can and we should aspire to know Him through faith. A perfected faith truly gives us contact with God and provides us with all the knowledge of Him which we are capable of receiving by means of our supernatural faculties and organism.

That is what we can say of God, in order to feed our contemplation.

II — GOD IS THE SOURCE OF ALL LIFE

God is the source of light and of love. We know that everything has come forth from Him, that all things have been created by Him. The apostle John tells us in his Prologue: "All things were made through Him and without Him nothing was made."[17] Here is something for us to exercise our minds on.

The creation of the world

How did God create? It is not easy to explain. There is a problem here, but for us it is resolved since creation is an article of faith. We do not have to explain *how*. The fact suffices for us: God has created.

Creation, a trace of God

We do know something of how God created things. He brought them into being by giving them a share in His own existence and also in His essence to a certain extent. The things He created are more or less perfect according to the degree in which they resemble Him and participate in His essence. He created matter, life, the angels.

God placed His signature upon all His creatures, even inanimate creation. As St. John of the Cross says, He left a "trace."[18] St. John of the Cross studies inanimate creation and finds there a trace of God: His footprint, His hand, His finger.

The breath of God

The creation of life and its burgeoning sprang one day from the energy of matter. But when God willed to place a spiritual soul within a creature, He did it by a new creative act. For matter, even energy, is neither infinite nor self-subsistent.

God had to breathe: "Let us make man in our image."[19] The creative act was precisely this breath of God which gave human beings their resemblance to Him: "Let us make man in *our* likeness." He gave us a soul which possessed an intellect and a will, already a likeness of God.

Now God could effect another creation, that is, He could plant, insert, graft onto this intellect and will, this natural soul, a higher good: grace, participation in His own life. God could not graft this onto an animal; a soul was required. This grace, participation in the life of God, is a living entity, a life which God has given, a sharing which makes us children of God.

Onto our faculties of intellect and will, God grafted the theological virtues, the infused virtues, a supernatural entity which would allow this grace to develop and advance toward its goal, to attain its full measure. It would enable the soul to perform divine operations, operations like those of God. Our being children of God would be incomplete without the accompanying operations. We were enabled to perform these operations through these faculties.

This, briefly, is the creation from which we emanate.

God's presence to His creation

As we know, God does not abandon creatures after making them. All flow from the "depths" of His love. *Bonum diffusivum*, and He does not abandon what He has made. He loves His handiwork, whatever it be, matter, life, man. He inserts Himself in it, He is present to it, even to matter. He gives it a destiny, a mission, a movement of return to God. Even matter, the apostle Paul tells us,[20] and in any case all life in this world, longs eagerly for the infinite One from whom it came forth. Creation groans in travail; it yearns for the end for which God created it, that is, for God Himself.

Presence of immensity

Where does this longing come from? Not from matter itself, nor from the animals, nor from life. It comes from the Spirit which is in this life, this matter.

Every creature is inhabited by God. God is present in it not only because He is infinite and fills all things; He is present in all His creation with the presence of immensity. It is He who directs all things and provides them with powers. He sustains creation; conservation is like an ongoing creation.

God is present in all atoms, cells, all parts of ourselves. In all spirit, all matter, God is present by His presence of immensity. This presence of immensity is active, especially in man.

The active presence of the Spirit

God is present to a far higher degree in persons endowed with grace. The Holy Spirit is given to us and at each instant this grace is increased by the Holy Spirit, by this Good diffusive of itself, and by substantial Love. He Himself is given to us, at the same time, in order that we may have a relationship with Him. This is God!

He is given to us, and it is He who breathes in us, He sighs toward the Infinite whence He comes. The Spirit makes us sigh for the infinite One. The filial Spirit within us aspires to the Father and aspires also, the saints tell us, to our Mother, the Virgin Mary. He sustains us, He wishes to raise us to this infinite One whence we came, this Father whose children we are through grace. It is the Spirit who carries us, who leads us. This is what God is!

The Spirit is our Guest, a living flame in us, a light. He is our friend. He is truly in us, He sanctifies us and divinizes us constantly. As we shall see, He wills to rule us by means of our faculties and His gifts, to reign over our intellect and our will. He aspires to royalty, to domination. His first presence, the presence accompanying the inpouring of grace in us, becomes gradually, we hope, thanks to our work and the discovery we make of Him, a presence of friendship. He becomes a friend, a beloved Guest from whom we want never to be separated.[21] Once we have found Him, we can no longer live without Him.

Presence of dominion

This presence of friendship which develops alongside our grace, our work of asceticism and our search for God, will become a presence of dominion. The Spirit becomes truly our master, our king, not only because of the homage we pay to Him, as to someone to whom we acknowledge our fealty occasionally, or to whom we make acts of consecration. No! Through an effective rule over our faculties He moves us, He truly acts through us.

This is what St. John of the Cross says. His affirmations are disconcerting, but are simply the consequence of the life of God and the existence of grace within us. And St. John of the Cross does not hesitate to tell us[22] that through the Holy Spirit and with Him we perform divine actions, acts emanating from our faculties but produced by the Spirit within us.

Here is a first gaze at God, God in Himself and God in us. This infinite, inaccessible, transcendent God wrapped in darkness remains so always, for He is no less infinite because He is within us. But He is *there*, within us.

The search for God

Let us remain gazing at God, let us renew this activity through faith, let us rediscover it. That is what our prayer is: we use the instruments we have in order to find God, to make contact with Him.

We shall examine this living organism of grace, this divinization of our soul by grace, in as much detail as possible. We shall look at each part, each device, each element of this organism in order to know it, to be fully aware of it, and to realize the treasure we possess.

Then we shall go on to consider how this spiritual organism functions. Ours will always be a theological study because it is God we are studying, and at the same time a psychological study, for the exercise includes both the activity of the grace which is given us, that supernatural instrument received at baptism, and the activity of our faculties. This makes the subject a rather delicate one. Psychology is intertwined with theology, and this can sometimes lead to confusion.

It is not always easy to distinguish the one from the other. St. Teresa sees this clearly; St. John of the Cross delights in it. Discerning it in a marvelous way, he quickly distinguishes one level from the other, sees them, recognizes them. We can succeed in doing this to some extent, progressively as he does. But in the beginning we may experience some confusion, because we are used to seeing things through their effects, studying them through our feelings and impressions.

We shall try to discern all this as far as possible in order to strengthen our faith and above all — and this is our practical goal — to develop a taste for God, for the exercise of the presence of God, the search for God. We shall then come to understand in a practical way that if eternal life consists primarily in seeing and possessing God, our life in this world already includes, as its principal exercise, the search for God and contact with Him. This is the principal, if not unique, occupation of our life in this world, and the exercise of eternal life, *inchoatio vitae aeternae*.[23] If we do not exercise it, if we do not develop our supernatural life, it will be deficient later when we come to see God. We shall only see and possess Him in heaven in proportion to the strength of the organism which we shall have developed here on earth.

Dominus tecum

Let us ask the Blessed Virgin, Our Lady of Life, who lived with God, for this. "*Dominus tecum*, the Lord is with you." This declaration of the angel implies an intimacy, a very close mutual relationship between God and Our Lady. She lives now in the glory of God and possesses Him. Let us ask her to teach us how to find God and live with Him, so that it can be true of us: *Dominus tecum*, the Lord is with us. What better witness could we bear than this?

May we ourselves say, in a certain sense, what our Lord said to Nicodemus: "No one goes to God of himself, only one bears witness to Him," and I, too, can bear witness. For although we have not been there, and are not like our Lord, in the unity of Persons, we can still invoke our experience of God sometimes, to affirm that it is possible and to give to others the taste and desire for it.

Notes

[1] *Summa theologica*, IIa IIae, q. 180, a. 3.

[2] *Ibid.*, a. 4.

[3] Cf. St. John of the Cross, *The Dark Night of the Soul*, 385-386, and *The Living Flame of Love*, str. 2, 595ff.

[4] Ex 3:14.

[5] Ps 102:28.

[6] Jn 1:1, 4.

[7] Ernest Psichari, French officer and writer (1883-1914). In the course of a long sojourn in Mauritania (1902-1912) he was converted to Catholicism; he intended to enter the Dominican Order but was killed by the enemy at the beginning of the war. He left two works in particular: *Appel des armes* [*The Call to Arms*],1913, and *Voyage du centurion* [*The Voyage of the Centurion*], published in 1916, which bear witness to his experience.

[8] The episode of the burning bush is found in Exodus, ch. 3.

[9] Cf. St. John of the Cross, *The Spiritual Canticle*, str. 13 and 14, 457-462; str. 32, 535-536.

[10] The meeting with Nicodemus is found in Jn 3:1-21.

[11] Cf. 1 Jn 1:1-3.

[12] Jn 3:16.

[13] Cf. Heb 1:3.

[14] Cf. Gn 1:31.

[15] Cf. St. Teresa of Avila, *The Interior Castle*, 7th Mansion, 430-431.

[16] In this world we cannot know the mystery of God and live in His presence except through faith. The latter is certain but obscure, for our intellects are not adapted to a clear, immediate vision of the divine mystery. In heaven God gives man, after his death, an immediate supernatural knowledge of Himself which allows him to see Him face to face as He is. This power of vision is called the *lumen gloriae* or light of glory.

[17] Jn 1:3.

[18] Cf. *The Spiritual Canticle*, str. 5, 434-435.

[19] Gn 1:26.

[20] Cf. Rm 8:19-23.

[21] Cf. Father Marie-Eugene, *I Want to See God*, vol. 2, 593.

[22] Cf. *The Living Flame of Love*, str. 3, 640ff.

[23] "The beginning of eternal life."

Baptismal Grace*

I — SPIRITUAL RICHES

I would like to keep our discussion on a purely spiritual plane. And yet I cannot avoid stressing, as we set out, that we are living in a world that is disturbed and anxious.... What is the cause of this disturbance and anxiety? You know as well as I; perhaps even better.

A disturbed, anxious world

New nations stand up and declare their desire for independence, perhaps even for dominance. Furthermore, in the world today powerful ideologies are spreading which apparently aim at destroying our ancient Christian civilization. These ideologies do not hide the fact that they have a new concept

* This text was published in part in: *"Un maître spirituel, le Père Marie-Eugène, o.c.d."* ["A spiritual master, Father Marie-Eugene, OCD"], *Carmel*, 1988/3-4, n. 51, 319-327.

of civilization and even of man. With their bewitching promises they seduce not only individuals, but huge masses of people hungry for happiness.... Although we may see only purely human aspirations at work throughout the world today, it is still quite possible that there is something more in these ideologies; namely, the action of the Evil Spirit, who would attack spiritual values and the Church which possesses them.

Faced with these threats, we are anxious, and perhaps our anxiety is legitimate. What lies ahead? Where will we be, where will our country be, and Europe, and the whole world, in fifteen or twenty years? It is extremely difficult to foresee. We feel that we will be living through unheard of events.

The lessons of history

Yet a more careful study of the past and the lessons it holds for us would show us that the history of the world and of nations is filled with similar upheavals. If we consider China or India, the most ancient civilizations, dating probably seven or eight thousand years before Christ, we see that their present civilization is pretty much the result of the upheavals these peoples suffered over the course of thousands of years: invasions, the influx of foreign hordes, and the establishment of oligarchies.

In the Near East we see one empire after another destroyed: the Medes, the Persians, the Greeks with Alexander, and then the Romans. Thanks to the semblance of order which the latter established throughout the world, Jesus could proclaim His message. The Incarnation had repercussions, as St. Paul would say; throughout the known world.[1]

Rome, converted by Christianity and becoming the champion of Christian civilization, herself underwent the assaults of those she had called barbarians. And these barbarians were in their turn won over to Christianity. Nations licked their wounds for a time; then undertook new research on God.... Philosophy, theology, and art came into ascendency in the thirteenth century and things seemed to be settling down once more, until this order was disturbed by new upheavals.

What is the lesson to be learned from these events?

The supremacy of the intellect

Naturally, there are several lessons in all this for us. First, there is the supremacy of the intellect. Throughout these shocks, upheavals, and struggles between civilizations, empires and cultures, we always find the keenest intellects dominating in the end. They may be overcome for a time, as Greek culture was overcome by the Roman empire, but they return and affirm their power. In these cosmic struggles intelligence comes out victorious. Superiority of intellect assures eventual supremacy.

The power of the Spirit

There is something more. The expansion of Christianity presents us with other powers, spiritual powers. Jesus came, and before dying, before suffering His apparently supreme defeat on Calvary, He said: "I have overcome the world. As for you, you will have to struggle, you will be conquered, you will be put to death, but have confidence: I have overcome the world."[2]

So we have supremacy of the intellect, supremacy of spiritual powers. Yes, the Church to which we belong will not succumb under blows, she will endure through all the upheavals, revolutions, transformations, and tidal waves from which they come, be they launched by all the powers of human intelligence and all the powers of hell. This is the conclusion we have to draw.

Inventory of our spiritual powers

In the anxiety in which we live, faced with these threats which are certain to materialize in some instances, what are we to do?

The great task, especially for Christians, is to make an inventory of our spiritual powers and place our hopes, not only those which we entertain for ourselves from a spiritual point of view but also our hopes for society, in these spiritual powers. Anxiety and disturbance must lead us to a deeper, stronger confidence in the spiritual powers which have been given to us. They must lead us toward what is spiritual, toward God. Herein lies the supreme hope for each one of us, for our own individual salvation and also for the salvation of humanity, insofar as it can be saved.

What are these spiritual powers, these riches? Let us make a brief inventory of them now, since the subject of this conference is "Baptismal grace." It is this above all that we need to explore, since it is the highest of our hopes.

Our great wealth

The first of our riches is our faith in God. Yes, we believe in God! Our God is subsistent Being, the infinite Spirit who knows neither beginning nor end. Our God is the Spirit of Love. We know that as Love, He lives in Himself, He engenders His Son, His light, His Word, the reflection of Himself. We know that the Father and the Son, knowing each other, breathe forth the Holy Spirit, the Spirit of Love.

God is the principle of all things, of everything that exists. He is the principle and the end. Why? Because He is Love; He created through love. He created inanimate nature and within it there is something of Himself, a faint trace as St. John of the Cross says.[3] In fact, this matter is energy. He created life, and in this life there is something which resembles Him still more closely, something of the power of His love. Above all these, through love God created man, the sum of all creation. In man He has put the breath of life, *spiraculum vitae*, the Bible tells us,[4] and this breath bears a resemblance to God.

Man is, of all creatures, beloved of God. God created man, and before creating him He thought of him, loved him. This is our treasure: God has loved us, He has created us in love, and because He loves us He wants to draw us back to Himself. His love is not satisfied with our creation. It will not be fully satisfied until we shall have returned to Him. This is our great treasure!

What are upheavals, threats, material forces, what are the powers of the mind even, compared with this loving thought of God, who created us that we might return to Him? Yes, this is our treasure, our hope: the thought of God, the love of God, which is not just a love for humanity in general but for each one of us individually.

How did God manifest this love? He gave Himself to be the end of every creature, and particularly our end. He did this by giving us a share in His life. This is the great act of God's love for man, in creation. Indeed, He has given us intellect and will, the resemblance to God found in the breath of life which He gave to the first man and which we also have. But His love is manifested supremely in what we call baptismal grace.

II — OUR BAPTISMAL GRACE

I would first like to study baptismal grace objectively in itself — ontologically, as the theologians say — and then psychologically, in its effects on our nature.

Created participation in the life of God

God created us through love, and in creating us through love He called us to Himself: He is our end. Even from a purely natural point of view we are made for Him. He loves us and places within our human nature a certain tendency toward Him, which is already a means of discovering and loving Him. He gives us the ability to know Him naturally, in creatures — enigmatically, indirectly, it is true[5] — and also to love Him. But through the grace we receive in baptism, we possess more than this.

What is this grace given to us in baptism? When the priest pours water on our head and says, "I baptize you in the name of the Father, and of the Son, and of the Holy Spirit," grace descends into our soul. What is this grace? A mysterious thing, as mysterious as God Himself. It is a created participation in God's life, in the nature of God.

What is God? The infinite One, subsistent Being.... Who can express this? When we are in heaven, with the help of the light of glory, the *lumen gloriae*,[6] we shall see something of Him, according to our power of vision. But here on earth, with our minds, how can we speak of such a thing? God is wrapped in light, a light so blinding that for us it becomes a robe of darkness!

Now grace is a created participation in the nature of God, in the life of God. It is not part of God. No, it is created, but it makes us children of God, it makes us like God. In a certain sense we can say that it makes us "God-made." Clearly, what it gives us lacks infinity, yet it is a participation in the life of God. This grace allows us to do works like God's works. We are not all-powerful or infinite, but it allows us to perform intellectual operations and works of love like God Himself, to enter into a relationship with Him and so to act like Him.

We cannot go further. Theology, sounding the depths of grace as it sounds the depths of God, will use philosophical language to try to express this reality. Such language will of course be not allegorical but analogical. We will say, "It is as if...."[7] We cannot express the thing in itself, but this is enough to show us the grandeur of grace.

Marked for Trinitarian life

In this energy, this life which is given to us — for it is life — there is a force, a power, an orientation. I said just now that in our natural human nature there is already a tendency toward God. He has marked us. This seal of the divine which we bear in our intellect and will is already an aptitude for knowing and loving God, and advancing toward Him in a sense. He is our end. Through grace, this seal is far more definite: there is a thrust toward Him, a yearning. Our natural longing for God can only be fully satisfied by grace.

This grace which is given to us, a participation in the life of God, marks our destiny. It dominates everything else in our human nature. It marks us for eternity. More than this, it marks us for God, for Trinitarian life. "I baptize you in the name of the Father, and of the Son, and of the Holy Spirit." In the naming of the three divine Persons lies our destiny, the description of our family. We are called to enter into the Trinity. These Persons are substantial relations in the unity of God. We are called to enter into the substantial relations of the Persons. One Person, the incarnate Word, has adopted us, and we are to enter through Him.

Grace calls us to this. It is made for this; herein alone lies its full realization. We are children of God, even here on earth under the veil of faith. This grace will not be fully clear to us until we shall have actually entered into the Blessed Trinity. Endowed then with the *lumen gloriae*, the power to see God, we can really enter into a relationship with God through knowledge and love, and enjoy these relationships. This is what grace is.

The grace in us determines our destiny, our heavenly and earthly vocation. For we are only here in this world in order to return to God, to develop this grace, to give it full scope and thus to reach the power of vision, the intimacy of relationship with the divine Persons, to which God has called us. In creating us, God saw us at the level of intimacy with Him. If He placed us in the world, it was so that we might return to Him, to the place destined for us in the mystical Body of Christ and in the Trinitarian life of the three divine Persons. This is what grace is.

What do the world's upheavals, revolutions, and ideologies matter? Or even the purely terrestrial transformations of the world, the galaxies which arise in the universe at every instant, the fruits of human intelligence, the hatred we sometimes feel around us? What do all the plots of the Evil Spirit matter, and his power in the world, when we possess within us this treasure, this participation in the life of God and this call to divine intimacy, to Trinitarian life?

We are quick to say that all this pertains to the transcendent, the "mystical" even. Perhaps we Christians sometimes confuse the transcendent, the mystical, with the unreal. No! This is reality! The transcendent and the mystical are not imaginary. They belong to eternal reality. We too are eternal in a certain sense, in the thought of God. God has willed what we are from all eternity, has loved us from all eternity. In loving us from all eternity in this way, He has had a thought about each one of us, a thought which He has realized, and He calls us to the perfect realization of His thought. God has created us for His eternity, for His joy and love, that He may delight in each of us and love us as He loves His Son, as He loves His Holy Spirit.

All earthly things, all natural things, all upheavals are as nothing in comparison with this! The peace we seek is here: in the tranquillity of this order we are to realize, in our advance toward God, in the harmony we are to realize in rediscovering the place and fulfilling the function for which God has destined us. This is true peace, beyond all else. Is there any other peace in this world? I do not know.... In any case, in the transcendent order there is no other than this. This is what grace is, baptismal grace.

Christian perfection is independent of all modalities, all human means, all natural perfections, whether sensory, intellectual, or even moral. Perfection for us, Christian perfection, consists in attaining to God. Our perfection is in God, it is union with God, and consequently it is the full development of our baptismal grace. It is nowhere else to be found; it is no other thing than this. All ways, methods, means, all forms of asceticism, should lead us to this.

Let us not confuse the means with the end. Perfection does not consist in some passing human perfection, in the development of our intellect, or even in moral perfection in itself. No! It consists solely in the fulfillment of our supernatural vocation, in the flowering of the grace given to us in baptism. It is nowhere else to be found.

This is the treasure which has been given to us by God: our faith in God, the relationship established between us and God through this reality which is grace, a participation in the life of God which orients us toward Him.

Grafted onto human nature...

What is grace on the psychological level? It is not some treasure, some jewel hidden in a corner of our soul. We might think, after reading St. Teresa,[8] that our soul is a casket in which we possess a gem which is God, is grace. No! This grace is set in our human nature. Man, the sum of creation, is material; he lives a sensory life as well as an intellectual life. This grace is engrafted onto the life of our soul, it is meant to complete, in a sense, our psychological being, to fix itself within our psychological being. Grace itself is in the essence of the soul. The theologian will tell us it is a "quality," that is, something accidental, but at the same time permanent.[9] It is another nature which comes to complete our purely natural nature. It is added over and above, and makes us children of God, God by participation.

All life is in motion and active. All life has organs in order to develop, members in order to move, to act. Thus we have within us sensory life and intellectual life. Like all life within us, our supernatural life, our grace, also has its members, its powers of action. How does it tend toward its end, its term, Trinitarian life? Precisely through its activity, the activity of its members, its faculties.

... *with powers for acting*

What are the members and faculties of the grace given us at baptism? They are the infused virtues of faith, hope, and love. They are called "infused" because they are a part of grace, they are not something super-added. Baptism, which gives us grace, also gives us the powers of acting and operating: the power of knowledge, which is faith, causing us to adhere to God; the power to move toward God, which is hope; and the power of union, which is charity.

This supernatural entity of baptismal grace is attached to the faculties of the soul. Faith is engrafted on the intellect, because the intellect has the power to know, or the power of intellection as the philosophers say. Grace too has its power to know, which is faith, and this faith is grafted on the intellect. Hope is grafted on the sensory powers. Charity, finally, the ruling power which impregnates all the others, an acting power, is grafted on the acting power of the soul which is the will or ruling faculty. Every human act is an act of the will. Every supernatural act implies an act of charity, the influence of charity. Thus, charity is grafted onto the will.

In this way our entire human being is completed by grace and becomes divine. This is our treasure.

Our advance toward God is thus accomplished both naturally and supernaturally. The supernatural does not exist in a pure state. There is no such thing as a purely supernatural action. Rising out of this union between the infused virtues, which are a part of grace, and the human faculties, every supernatural action necessarily includes some activity of these human faculties. Scholars have long sought to find out what an act of pure love is. They wanted to detach it completely from the human element in order to purify it. That is a myth! There is no such thing as an act of pure love separated from an act of the will, and consequently from the imperfections of the will.

Our journey toward God, therefore, is not made solely through the activity of our supernatural powers, our baptismal grace. It is made by our whole being, our whole soul tending toward God. All our energies, even our sensory energies, have their part in it. It is a journey of divinized persons toward their end, toward the summit.

Our Christian perfection

This is the spiritual life, this is the journey of human persons wholly sanctified, divinized, elevated by grace and by the infused virtues which have been given to them, so supernaturalized that already their acts are acts of the Trinitarian life. Because of the grace and virtues which dominate and impregnate them, inspire and divinize them, all the acts of the sensory faculties and the intellect are complete acts.

Human perfection, Christian perfection, is present in this journey toward the goal, toward God; it is present in the activity of the powers and energies at all levels as they move toward God. The whole person must arrive at the goal: no part is excluded.

These are our privileges. This is what has been given to us at baptism. We need to have clear ideas about it. The concept of Christian perfection has been obscured by methods and means which are for the most part excellent but which remain secondary. Asceticism, or virtue, or solitude, are sometimes given priority.... In the first centuries, people left the cities for the desert, the Thebaid. Stylites, striving for perfection, climbed up columns to preach at the gates of cities. People chose one or another text of the Gospel, believing that perfection lay in that.... No! There is only one Christian perfection, only one perfection of the human person divinized by baptismal grace. It is our journey to God, our getting lost in God, our plunge into God.

And the death we fear, the suffering which terrifies us, what do they matter? They bring us closer to our end! This death which frightens us is necessary if we are to enter into the life of God. We only plunge into God through the rent in the veil, that veil which is our body, our life in this world. St. John of the Cross will say: "Tear the veil of our sweet encounter."[10] It is death he is calling to, in calling for union with God. The plunge into God is made only through death.

Our great hope

Our great hope is our baptismal grace. We need to be aware of this reality. It is absolutely necessary that we be conscious of this treasure which we have been given, which we possess. Our great treasure is our baptismal grace. We must value it rightly, above all else. It determines our eternal destiny and throws its light on the path we should follow in this world, the furrow we are meant to plow. Let us not be led astray by other truths, whose importance and necessity I do not deny, but which sometimes risk overshadowing this great truth, leaving this treasure in darkness.

Someone may say: "This is all very well for contemplatives!" What do we all want to do, ultimately, if not contemplate God? Where do we want to go, if not where we can see God? What is heaven, what is the point of this life, if not to gaze at God and lose ourselves in Him, our source and our end? It is not only contemplatives who need to be aware of these realities and to think about them. This is for every Christian, all the baptized, all human beings.

You know, you appreciate this baptismal grace. I am not telling you anything new. I am simply emphasizing supernatural truths which you already know and esteem. I would like to place them in relief, in the full light of day, so that the eyes of your faith may consider them more attentively, more often; so that the esteem you have for them may be reasonable and proportioned to their value. These truths are a light to guide your enthusiasm, your love for God. They will feed your hope and strengthen it throughout your lives.

Once we are aware of our baptismal grace, the seal it confers, the light it gives, the orientation it insures, and the hope it bestows, we have an anchor in life for our soul. It seems as if despair cannot touch us any more, and all our anxieties are quieted. God loves me, God gives me His grace, God calls me. He is my hope. What more do I need? Of course my sensory nature may shudder, my intellect may be troubled at certain perspectives, but I possess the great hope!

The great hope is God Himself, whom I must reach. It is God Himself who calls me to turn and make my way back to Him. It is He who wants me to reach Him. Why? For His own delight. If I can find my joy only in Him, He too finds His joy in me.

This is what our baptismal grace is: the object of our faith, the support of our hope, love's food.

Notes

[1] Cf., for example, Eph 1:9-10 and Col 1:15-20.

[2] Cf. Jn 16:33.

[3] Cf. St. John of the Cross, *The Spiritual Canticle*, str. 5.

[4] Gn 2:7.

[5] Cf. 1 Cor 13:12.

[6] Cf. "The Mystery of God," n. 16.

[7] On analogical language, see "Prayer as Contact with God," 59.

[8] Cf. St. Teresa of Avila, *The Interior Castle*, 1st Mansion.

[9] Cf. Father Marie-Eugene, *I Want to See God*, vol. 1, 26-27 and vol. 2, 586-587.

[10] Cf. St. John of the Cross, *The Living Flame of Love*, str. 1.

Part Two — Toward Transformation in Love

Prayer as Contact with God

Long ago St. Augustine wrote: "You have made us for yourself, O Lord, and our hearts are restless until they rest in you."[1] The truth is that we come from God, and are on our way back to Him. Human nature carries within it a tendency stemming from its origin and Creator. It yearns to return to its master and end, who is God.

Many people are not fully aware of this tendency, this orientation to God. Yet this yearning of human nature is real. At periods of crisis like the present, when the world seems invaded by materialism and a prey to profound disturbances and fears for the future, this yearning surfaces and grows in intensity, even though those who rarely or never descend into the depths of their souls may remain unconscious of it. Today the increasing power of this yearning is observable. A sure indication of it is the growing interest in spirituality.

We are oriented toward God, we are returning to God. How can we citizens of this world, especially we Christians, make contact with God? In this contact with God, what is our part? These are questions I would like to discuss with you, on the basis of the revealed truth which is given to us and explained by the Church. I depend also upon psychological truth and on the spiritual doctrine of the masters of Carmel who are, so to say, specialists and professionals in the search for God.

What is prayer?

First let us see what we think about prayer, what the word evokes. For most people the word "prayer" suggests a religious act, the recitation of vocal petitions to God. For artists and poets it connotes a certain religious feeling, a sensation experienced in the deepest and noblest part of ourselves, an emotion which seems to bring with it a certain contact with God. For at least some philosophers, prayer is a passage beyond external things, the sensible world, and even beyond the intellectual domain, a passage which leads us further into the realms of the spirit. We know that certain modern philosophers see in this exploration, this more profound awareness of themselves, a discovery of God.

For the mystic also, prayer is a passage beyond, a search for God which is affirmed by profound impressions and a mystical religious experience, in which human activity has its part but the action of God predominates.

Each of these definitions contains some truth, but needs to be developed and completed. And it seems to me that for this, all we have to do is turn to the catechism definition and study it in depth.[2] What is prayer? Prayer is "the lifting up of the soul to God." Take away, if you will, the words "lifting up." Prayer is the movement of our whole self, our person, toward God. Prayer is making contact with God in order to converse with Him; it is a conversation, or as St. Teresa will say, "an affectionate exchange."[3]

Clearly love is the foundation of union, of the exchange. Love is the source of our movement; it is also the end, for the one who loves wants to love still more. And love is at the same time the bond which forms the union.

I — APPROACHING GOD

In this prayer which is an approach to God, an exchange with Him, what happens?

The presence of the infinite God

Let us first ask where this God is whom we seek. We are going to God, so we need to know where He is. We know that God is everywhere, because He is infinite. He is in the created world not only as Creator but also as Preserver. All things exist only through the action of God, through His presence. God is simple Being. He acts everywhere, and wherever He acts, He is present.

To go to God, then, is to seek within ourselves, or in nature, or in creation, or beyond the created world in the realm of possibilities, in the limits of creation and in the infinite beyond, to seek this living Being who is God. For God is not a thing; God is a living Being.

The catechism teaches us that God is infinite, and that in this infinite Being there are three Persons: the Father who engenders His Son, the Father and the Son who, knowing each other and finding each other perfect, love each other and by a common spiration produce the Holy Spirit, the common spiration of Father and Son, the spiration of Love personified. For us therefore, God is a living Being. Allow me to insist upon this truth, for we often misunderstand it, and modern errors about prayer and about the search for God go astray on this point.

God is a living Being, an infinite Being distinct from us. God is an infinite Being, we are finite.

Between us, who are creatures, between our person and God, there is infinity, an infinite space, a distance. It is not a ditch, but a chasm. Whether we seek this infinite Being within ourselves or in creation or beyond it, God, the living Being who penetrates us and all creation, is still, so to speak, separated from us by this infinity.

The problem of prayer is to move toward God, to cover this infinite distance between God and ourselves. Can we do it? If you will, let us try to approach God, to pray somehow, and at the same time to analyze briefly the activities going on within us.

You will forgive me for these philosophical and psychological digressions. It is good, from time to time, or at least once in our lives, to observe what we are doing when we set out to pray. We do not do this merely for the sake of speculative knowledge, but in order to perfect our prayer by perfecting all the movements and activities which have a part in our search for God.

Postures, attitudes at prayer

When I set out to pray, I must begin somewhere. I might not go to church. I might not seek God in the tabernacle or in some house of prayer. I might decide instead to pray at home. But even at home, there is bound to be some kind of physical motion on my part. At the very least, I will set aside my ordinary activities, whatever I may happen to be doing. Perhaps I will kneel down. The reason for this is my innate feeling that if I want to pray really well, I should let my external senses have their part in the prayer. There are a number of postures, or attitudes, generally considered appropriate for prayer, such as kneeling, standing with arms extended or raised, etc. A study of art in different countries, particularly primitive art such as we find in the catacombs, shows us a variety of positions taken by persons at prayer.

Postures vary with peoples, cultures, and our ideas of God, but everywhere we find external attitudes associated with prayer. Today, in order that people may share more integrally in the Sacrifice of the Mass, definite positions are suggested during the celebration, and rightly so, because in the context of our civilization certain attitudes express certain sentiments.

We stand during the *Creed* because standing expresses an attitude of confession, affirmation. We kneel during the Consecration because kneeling denotes adoration, and we are adoring the mystery of transubstantiation and the presence of Christ on the altar. Thus we are praying with our external attitude, with our bodies. In the approach to God which is prayer, in the making of the contact, our external attitude is our first contribution.

The activity of the interior faculties

But we haven't arrived at prayer yet. It is not enough to kneel down. There is work to be done by the interior faculties, imagination and memory. Let us suppose that I am in church or at home and I am seeking God. I place myself in front of a picture or before the Crucifix, and my memory recalls the sacrifice of Calvary. Or perhaps I am in church, kneeling before the tabernacle. Again, my memory brings to mind a truth I learned in the catechism: Jesus is present here, body, blood, soul and divinity.

On the other hand, I may try to represent this presence with the help of my imagination. I know well that imagination cannot produce the reality. It can only do its own work, namely, it can create images which will represent the truth symbolically. It reconstructs reality in its own mode.

I engage in these activities in order to occupy my senses of memory and imagination with the truth. These faculties can only be engaged and held by images. It seems to me that this kind of activity is necessary for my prayer, because if I do not occupy my memory and imagination they dart off in all directions, they become engrossed in other things, and I am unable to continue my prayer.

But now we come to the question of making contact with God. My imagination and memory do not produce this contact. They can only create images. When I want to recall a beloved person who is far away, and I pick up his photograph or try to remember his features, all I succeed in producing is symbols. I have not made a living contact with my friend. For living contact I need his presence. I must be able to speak with him, touch him. My affection must truly reach him, if a living exchange is to be established.

How shall I contact God in this way, how realize a living contact with Him? I have my intellect: God is spirit, and I too am spirit; I have my soul which is a spirit. Can I establish contact with God in this way, can my spirit touch the spirit of God?

St. John of the Cross, an expert on the subject of prayer, replies: No, this is not possible.[4] I can make this kind of contact with another human person, as I am doing with you right now. I have a thought in my mind which I represent with a word, and thanks to this word which I articulate, the thought in my mind penetrates your mind. Between us there is now a real communication of mind and thought. Can I do this directly with God? No, because I am not on the same level with God.

The communication which you and I are able to establish between us is possible because both our intellects are finite. The thought present in my mind, represented by my words, can enter your mind because our minds have, so to say, the same quality. Both are finite. But with God, we encounter the infinite. We are finite beings with limited capacity and our intellects, however brilliant, are finite and cannot attain to God, who is infinite. We are blocked by the distance, the lack of proportion.

The language of analogy

We know well that God has willed to establish this communication between Himself and us. He sent us His Incarnate Word, who told us what takes place in the heart of God. Our Lord said clearly to Nicodemus, "No one can speak of God, of the life of God, except the One who has come. He knows what takes place there."[5] And Christ brings us this truth.

But the language used by Jesus, the Incarnate Word, and by the Church to whom He gave the mission of teaching us, can only be "analogical." God cannot express Himself in human words because human speech is finite and He is infinite. Just as the ocean cannot be contained in a glass, so and with greater reason the infinite cannot be contained and expressed in human words and language, which are adapted only to thought.

In order to tell us something of what takes place in this mysterious and infinite Being, Jesus used analogical language. He translated the infinite, which human language is unable to contain, into human language. In the same way — and again this is a comparison — someone who comes from a foreign land where he has seen extraordinary things, and who wants to describe them to us, resorts to similitudes. He describes an animal by saying that its head is like this, its body like that; in a word, he makes comparisons, in an attempt to convey something of what he has seen. He uses symbolic, analogical language.

With regard to the infinite, our Lord acted in the same way. He spoke of things we know, things adapted to our thought, realities we are familiar with, and used these things to translate infinite truth into language we could know and understand. He made use of things which lay within our experience and intellectual capacity. In this way He imparted to us the truths of dogma which we find in our catechism. The truths expressed are analogical truths. The expression is the most perfect possible, and cannot be changed. Yet in itself the expression is not perfect.

Since the expression is not perfect, we cannot, through this expression, establish complete union with God. We need still another means.

Contact through faith

Shall we ever be able, then, to cross this vast distance and establish communication with God, make contact with Him and have an exchange? Yes, it is possible. God has given us a way. Not only has He given us truth, but He has given us, beyond all else, grace, divine life. We are God by participation. We are the children of God.

In baptism Christians receive a means, an instrument, a power. The supernatural virtue of faith allows us to truly establish contact and union with God, to cross the distance between the infinite God and ourselves. In order to seek this God present within us or in the tabernacle, we have the virtue of faith. It is an incomparable treasure, for it enables us to reach God. In baptism we receive supernatural life, and like all life it has within it powers of motion and development.

We have our physical life and a body with members and organs which enable it to develop, move, and act. We have the life of our soul, and with this life we are given faculties, intellect and will, which enable it to grow and develop. In the same way the supernatural life given to us in baptism can act, develop, flower. It has the means to do this. It has, so to speak, members, faculties, and powers which enable it to act, to perform actions proper to the supernatural life, and to develop.

The first faculty which we possess, the first power, is precisely the virtue of faith which enables us to penetrate God, to enter into God.

How shall I perform this act of faith which we

liken to prayer? I will take a truth which has been given to me, for example "one God in three Persons." This is a human, analogical expression of the truth which is in God. I recall it with my senses. I have read it, I have heard it, and I present it to my intellect. My mind examines it, ponders it and sees that there is no contradiction in it: "Three Persons, a single nature in God."

My intellect, however, does not accept it. Why not? Because my intellect can only be moved to accept a truth when it appears self-evident. Two and two make four: this is a self-evident truth, and my intellect accepts it. But "three Persons in one God"? There is no contradiction here, but there is not the light, the evidence which would oblige me to accept it, to acknowledge that it is true.

Confronted with a truth which is not self-evident, I naturally look for the authority behind it, for I know well that I cannot by myself know everything through external or internal evidence. I accept and believe many things only because they have been told to me by someone, and the evidence supplied seems sound. That is witness. I have never seen America, but they say it exists, and I have such proofs of the credibility of this statement that I believe as firmly in the existence of America as if I had seen it. That is witness.

This truth, "one God in three Persons," which is not self-evident to me, is affirmed by the Church.

I investigate whether the Church has the authority to make this statement, and whether this affirmation is part of the deposit of truths left to the Church by Christ. I discover that the Church has the authority to speak in the name of God, and now I have a witness. I have done my intellectual work, I have made an enquiry, and I say to myself, "Since this is affirmed by God, I should believe it."

What happens now that I know I should believe? Admitting this, my intellect now abdicates, so to speak. It recognizes that it can go no further and that it is obliged to adhere although it does not understand. I do not put my faith in evidence which I perceive, therefore. For the moment I am putting my faith in the power, the truth of the witness. When I reach this point, at this moment, I make an act of faith. I say, "My God, I believe that you are, I believe that you exist, and that in you there are three Persons." That is the "Act of Faith."

What has happened? Thanks to the submission of my intellect, which has recognized that it can go no further and that nonetheless it ought to adhere; thanks to this reasonable submission, *obsequium rationabile*, as the apostle Paul calls it,[6] my intellect, having done all it is capable of and recognizing that there is only one thing it can now reasonably do, adheres to the truth which is proposed to it. Is this an act of faith? Not yet.

Like a graft...

The act of faith consists in a positive movement, an act of the virtue of faith which was given to us in baptism. This virtue of faith is grafted upon our intellect as the graft is on the vine stock. We know what the vine-dresser does when he grafts the vine: he prunes the stock, makes a cut and inserts the graft whose fruit he wishes to produce. The graft is attached, and after a few weeks or months it will be incorporated in the vine stock. Henceforth the vine-dresser will have the roots of the original vine, the original stock, and attached to this stock a graft of the quality he desires for the fruits to come.

In our souls we have senses, which bring nourishment to our intellect. The intellect is like the original vine stock. On this original vine stock, the intellect, we have the graft of faith. The supernatural does not exist in what we might call its pure state in us. It is grafted onto our human nature, our human faculties. The intellect receives faith. Faith cannot act without the intellect.

Faith acts with the light coming to it through both intellect and senses, just as the graft on the vine receives sap through the original stock and through the roots buried in the earth. But the graft of the vine bears its own fruit, not that of the original stock. Similarly, in the soul faith will produce its own proper act which is not an act of the intellect but an act of the virtue of faith, a supernatural act.

Just now we said that the intellect, by its own power, cannot penetrate into God, because it is finite and God is infinite. But this virtue of faith which has been given to us in baptism, insofar as it is a supernatural, divine medium, can penetrate into God. It penetrates the divine essence, it *really* enters there. This is its function. The advantage of our supernatural organism is now apparent. It really penetrates God, it performs an act of knowledge, a penetration into God.

The essential act of prayer

Here we come to the essential act of prayer, which it is important to stress. When we pray, when we make an act of faith, relying on an affirmation of truth in the catechism, and use a customary prayer formula such as those used at Mass, we enter into God. We establish direct contact, a profound, living contact with God.

Just now we were asking how we could grasp the infinite. We grasp it *by faith*. How I wish we could comprehend the incomparable value of our faith! Faith not only benefits our souls by enlightening us about the essence of God and all the other truths we could never attain solely by our intellect. It also puts us *in contact with God*, a supreme benefit.

For this is what prayer is: contact with God.

In the Gospel we see at almost every moment the effect of faith in Jesus' relationships with the crowds or with persons who come to ask Him for a grace. When anyone comes to our Lord to ask for a miracle, He generally asks, "Do you believe?"[7] That is to say, "Are you truly in contact with me, do you have a relationship with me, with the divinity within me, with the power of my divinity?" And once the contact is established, the miracle is worked.

It even happens at times that there is no dialogue between our Lord and the person who comes to ask for a grace. Consider for example the woman of Capernaum with the hemorrhage. Drawing near to Jesus, she says to herself, "If only I might so much as touch the hem of his garment, I should be healed."[8] In fact, she does touch the tassel of our Lord's cloak *with faith*, and immediately feels herself cured. And our Lord turns around. "Who touched me?" The Apostles say to him, "Everyone is crowding against you, and you ask who touched you!" Yes, but someone has touched Him, it is faith that touched Him; it pierced Him like a sword, and drew forth power from Him.

Just as the Canaanite woman[9] who beseeches Him with faith, and the centurion who prays with faith,[10] cause our Lord to thrill with joy, so the woman with the hemorrhage produces a vibration in Christ. The centurion elicits His enthusiasm: "Never have I found such faith in Israel. . . ."[11]

This enthusiasm, this vibration which we sense in Christ, we too may produce in God Himself each time we touch Him with ardent faith. There we have it: the contact of prayer, the value of prayer, the very *essence* of prayer. We know, certainly, that prayer has its outward forms and that it includes recollection and thought. But basically it is *contact with God*.

This contact is penetrating, and when we penetrate God, when the contact is established, there is a real exchange. God is an ocean, a fire, a living fountain. Each time we make contact with God we touch the ocean that He is, the flame that He is, and consequently we draw from Him the divine substance. We receive an increase in that participation in divine life which is the grace within us.

It may be that we do not obtain the particular temporal favor we have asked for, but we receive something much better, because we are divinized by contact with God. That is the essence of prayer: this contact with a living God, a God who reacts, not like a simple inanimate being but like a *living person*, with a thrill of joy, with the gift of Himself.

II — THE MOST HUMAN OF ALL ACTIONS

Prayer, this contact with God, takes on many different forms. It is an exercise of the virtue of faith, and can be performed by everyone who possesses faith. It will naturally assume different outward forms, but essentially it will be the same for all: it will always be this contact between the living Being who is God and our souls, through faith. Yet externally it may have many different aspects.

An awakened faith

Can a child pray? Yes, of course. How will she express her prayer? As a child does, by throwing a kiss to the tabernacle, by a smile perhaps, by a word we can hardly understand — but what does it matter? She expresses her prayer as she can. And since she has faith, and has been told that Jesus is in the tabernacle or within herself, she is able to exercise her faith, not articulately like an adult, but still authentically.

The contact is established with God and in consequence the enrichment of the contact is realized in the child. A little later, she will make contact through images, then through thought. But this contact, whatever its external form, will be according to the measure of her faith.

In our prayer, let us be careful to make this contact and to keep our faith alert. Our exercise of prayer will perhaps be vocal, but it should be animated interiorly by faith, by an act of the faith that is in us. This may be elicited at times by meditation or by silence.

People too often think that prayer, to be fervent, efficacious, and penetrating, must be supported with a great deal of external or intellectual activity. This is not true. Even in a state of fatigue in which I can no longer command my faculties, and cannot think, a state which leaves me indifferent — provided that the virtue of faith within me seeks God, speaks its trust and love to God, my prayer will be efficacious.

Prayer is *always* possible, simply because the soul can always make this interior act of faith.

We are made for God

We know that our prayer, being always possible, can become continual once we have formed the habit. Our prayer should be, at least in tendency and desire, as continual as possible.

What is a Christian? A Christian is of course someone whose faith is affirmed through charity, outward behavior, the accomplishment of duties. But essentially, Christians tend toward their end,

God. Christians believe that they come from God and are returning to God, that they are called to participate in the divine life, and to lose themselves in the Blessed Trinity. Christians truly believe this. They believe that their true life is not here below but in the Blessed Trinity. For we are *made for God*, we are made for heaven, and heaven does not consist solely in finding our loved ones once more. The essence of heaven is the discovery of God, and entrance into the rhythm of the Blessed Trinity.

Grace makes us children of God and, in the heart of the Blessed Trinity are the Father, Son, and Holy Spirit. Our grace calls us precisely to identify ourselves with the Word of God, the Son of God. The Son of God became incarnate. It is in Him that we find our end. We should strive to lose ourselves in Him. And it is in Him that we shall find our happiness, which will be to be identified with Him, to enter with Him into the Blessed Trinity, to share its works and thus its happiness. This is our end, this is heaven: not only to behold God, but to act with God by acting with the Word, the Son of God. This is our end, the life that has no end, the life of heaven.

Prayer, contact with God, is already the exercise of eternal life. It is the exercise of heaven, the realization of the works we shall perform there. Our life in this world has been given to us only that we might prepare for heaven, exercising ourselves, doing here and now what we shall be doing in heaven.

We do this in faith, that is to say without great enjoyment. In heaven we shall do it with vision, and in perfect happiness.

Prayer therefore is not something incidental in our life. It is the Christian act par excellence, the preparation for our eternity, the realization in advance of what we shall be doing in eternity.

The power of prayer

When we consider prayer in this light, as a contact with God which is the essential human act — the human act par excellence because it is already a divine act — we see the importance it should have in our life. I am not speaking here of the power of prayer from the point of view of the grace we can receive, but of its power insofar as it associates us with the life, and consequently the power, of God.

It is God who directs the world, and we have a means of participating in this power of God and hence in the direction of the world with Him. It is through prayer, through contact with Him, by joining ourselves to Him and uniting ourselves to Him, that we in our turn, with Him, may direct the world, so to speak. St. Teresa tells us that the soul who prays in union with Him takes turns with God in ruling the world.[12] God allows that soul to govern the world at His own moments and times. Or rather, the soul is entirely subject to God, but God, who never allows Himself to be outdone in thoughtfulness, gives the soul its turn in the government of the world.

When we shall be in heaven and shall see things in truth, we shall be struck by seeing how delicately God has dealt with us and with all the souls which were united with Him, allowing them governance of the world and even yielding to their desires in the direction of events. Prayer, as St. Thérèse of the Child Jesus will say,[13] is like a queen, like a power entering into the heart of God and sharing in the government of the world.

It has sometimes been said that a prayerful soul is an egoist who seeks delight in prayer and leaves the world to itself. How unfortunate are those who say this, for they have not understood, even though they are Christians, what prayer really is! No, the way to be concerned for the world and to practice charity toward it — oh, there are other ways, and I am not saying this is the only one — but the most effective way ultimately is to enter into the movement of God through prayer.

Let us, if you will, remember this: prayer leads us into God, it lets us make contact with Him, and if it is perfect it makes us share at the same time in His works. Let us recall that this means is always available to us. Day and night, through an act of faith, we can enter into Him, rest in Him. Let us remember that God's door is always open to us, and we can enter into Him through prayer. God is a consuming fire, an ever-flowing fountain. He is the Good diffusive of itself, and consequently at each instant it only depends on us, through an act of faith, an act of love, to make contact with Him, to vivify and enrich ourselves spiritually.

It depends on us to perform this divine act that is prayer, to enter into God, and when we are in Him, to act on this First Cause by the contact we have established and by the love we bear Him and which He bears us. We are enabled to act in and through Him for the good of our own souls and of the world.

Let us rest simply with these thoughts, especially that of contact with God, and let us profit by this truth. I should like to see it sink deep into your souls, there to become a dominant idea, a thought that will plunge you into true life, into God. Plunged thus in God, at least from time to time, may you experience more and more the desire to return there, to live with Him, and in this contact with Him to be divinized, to become a power for those around you and for the world.

Notes

[1] St. Augustine, *Confessions*, Book 1.

[2] I am speaking of the traditional catechism definition: "Prayer is the lifting of the soul to God to adore Him, thank Him, ask His forgiveness and obtain His graces."

[3] St. Teresa of Avila, *Life*, ch. 8, 67.

[4] St. John of the Cross, *The Ascent of Mount Carmel*, II, 8, 125: "This chapter shows in a general manner how no creature or knowledge comprehensible to the intellect can serve it as a proximate means for the divine union with God."

[5] Cf. Jn 3:11-14.

[6] Cf. Rm 12:1.

[7] For example, the two blind men in Mt 9:27-29; the paralytic in Lk 5:20; Martha, the sister of Lazarus in Jn 11:26.

[8] Mk 5:28.

[9] Cf. Mt 15:21-28.

[10] Cf. Mt 8:5-13.

[11] Mt 8:10.

[12] St. Teresa of Avila, *The Way of Perfection*, ch. 33, 164; see also Father Marie-Eugene, *I Want to See God*, vol. 2, 662-667.

[13] Cf. *Manuscript C*, 25 r°.

The Activity of God in Prayer

Prayer is contact with God. We establish it through the exercise of the virtue of faith which is received in baptism and is a part of our supernatural organism. This activity of faith, however, cannot be exercised without the intellect, whose activity is in turn subordinated to that of the senses. The contact with God which is prayer is thus brought about by the activity of both natural and supernatural faculties.

This contact of faith causes us to penetrate the depths of God, the essence of God. It allows us to draw from Him light, life, and an increase of grace, which is already an appreciable result. However this contact still remains imperfect, or at least it cannot be maintained, since it depends on the activity of our human faculties, which are imperfect. At this point, in order to perfect the activity of the virtue of faith, God intervenes with His own activity. God intervenes in our prayer.

Prayer is not a monologue. It is a common error to say that in order to pray, it is enough to think of God, to make an act of faith, and to establish contact, and that in doing this we make a perfect prayer. God is indeed good, but He is infinite Being, and consequently far above us. Doubtless faith succeeds in crossing over this distance which separates us from Him. But — and this is the common, very widespread error — God only intervenes in our prayer from time to time, so runs the argument, and in a way we cannot precisely express.

This is the practical error underlying many purely natural teachings on contemplation. It is something we should react against. I should like to talk with you about God's activity in prayer, and try to show something of the mechanism as well as the effects of His intervention.

I — THE INTERVENTION OF GOD THROUGH THE GIFTS

The darkness of mystery

When the soul has made contact with God through faith, it does indeed find God, but for the intellect and the natural faculties there is only darkness. It is true that faith is a light, but a light, as we saw in the last conference, which nourishes our intellect with truth formulated in analogous terms,[1] truth which we cannot penetrate. The essential object of faith is obscure.

As a result of this our faculties, finding themselves confronted with mystery and obscurity, quickly grow weary. This is the reason for the distractions and fatigue of prayer. Let us suppose that I start to pray. I recite some vocal prayer which feeds my mind. I can also nourish my prayer with meditation on some dogmatic truth or some aspect of the life of our Lord in the Gospel. But soon my senses grow weary, and show their fatigue by distraction. They turn to other objects. Even my intellect, made for light, cannot resign itself to the obscurity. It does not understand, and seeks diversion in objects offering it greater clarity. It returns to its usual preoccupations, which are sources, again, of distraction and fatigue in prayer.

The result is this: after having prayed for a few minutes, I feel that my prayer is futile. I find that I am not in control of my faculties. They want no more to do with prayer, and turn to other things, and I stop praying. It is now that God's activity intervenes.

Receptive antennae: the gifts of the Holy Spirit

How does God intervene? We saw above that each time we make contact with God through faith, we are enriched by more grace, by the divine substance — not by the uncreated divine substance,

God Himself, but by that divine reality which is grace, a participation in the life of God. This is not the only fruit of this contact and prayer. God intervenes directly at the psychological level, that is, where my faculties are at work, to perfect my prayer.

How does He intervene? Through the gifts of the Holy Spirit. In our supernatural make-up we have grace properly so called, which is grafted upon the essence of our soul. This makes us children of God, God by participation. We have the theological virtues and the infused moral virtues,[2] which are principles of activity like organs, the members of our supernatural life, of our grace.

The catechism teaches us that we also receive the gifts of the Holy Spirit. Few Christians are familiar with the teaching on the gifts of the Holy Spirit. They are partially excusable for this, in fact completely excused, for theologians venture only with the greatest caution into an explanation of the gifts of the Holy Spirit. This subject presents difficulties not only from the dogmatic point of view, but more particularly from the psychological aspect. Let me try to throw some light on the problem.

The gifts of the Holy Spirit, which are part of our supernatural organism, are not powers of activity like the virtues, but receptive organs, receptive antennae so to speak. Just as antennae capture Hertzian waves, so the gifts of the Holy Spirit, which are part of our supernatural organism, can and do serve effectively to capture the divine waves sent forth by God.

These gifts of the Holy Spirit are not superior to the virtues, which are active powers. The virtues of faith, hope and charity, entering into direct contact with God, into the very essence of God, cannot be surpassed. There is nothing higher than them. But the gifts of the Holy Spirit are given to perfect the virtues in their exercise.

Just now, appealing to your practical experience of prayer, I said that when we pray, when we make contact with God by an act of faith, adoration, or love, or by some vocal prayer which facilitates these supernatural acts, we soon become weary. Our senses are fatigued at feeling nothing; our intellect, made for clarity, is also soon fatigued by seeing nothing and not finding its normal nourishment which is pure truth, for which it was created and to which it is adapted. Thus the virtue of faith grafted onto the intellect falls back, because the intellect which serves as its support at the base of its activity has itself turned away from its object. The contact is lost.

It is now that the action of God intervenes through the gifts of the Holy Spirit. These antennae, the gifts of the Holy Spirit, are grafted, if we want to locate them from a psychological viewpoint, at the intersection of the supernatural virtues and the faculties. What they seek to receive from God, the divine wave lengths which are going to reach them, pass through this intersection of the theological virtues, the infused virtues, and the faculties to which they are attached.

Let us take for example the virtue of faith. The action of God through the gifts of the Holy Spirit is going to reach the summit of the intellect, there where the point of contact is made between the intellect and faith. And what is going to happen? In this realm we can only appeal to the experience of contemplative souls and theologians.

A theologian like St. Thomas[3] will tell us that three gifts of the Holy Spirit are contemplative gifts: knowledge, understanding, and wisdom. Each has a particular mission, a special function. Let me hasten to add that this distinction between the gifts might be called superficial, since it does not get to the bottom of things. However it is helpful in clarifying our problem.

Quieting of the senses: the gift of knowledge

When we begin to pray, our senses are first wearied by not perceiving anything. Faith has penetrated into God but God is a mystery, obscurity. God intervenes here through the gift of knowledge: this antenna will bring perceptions to the interior and exterior senses.

What is the result of this action of God?

Calmness in the senses. There is an impression of peacefulness, which may be either pleasant or painful, but still it is a quieting which may go so far as a certain ligature of the faculties, the senses. But the painful quieting or ligature of the senses allows our faith to rest in God.

Quieting perceptions: the gift of understanding

To this action of God through the gift of knowledge is normally added His action through the gift of understanding. This gift, which is not understanding itself but another antenna, brings supernatural clarity to the understanding. The clarity may be distinct, enlightening the understanding on a specific point or truth. There may even be, in certain cases, lights about the future, extraordinary lights. But usually these lights of God coming through the gift of understanding and thus acting upon the natural human faculty of understanding, are transcendent lights which blind it. They furnish it with a certain clarity but keep it in darkness. They have however the advantage of setting the intellect at rest, penetrating it to its depths, and arresting its reasoning activity.

We have in our intellect a reasoning power, and in addition to this something more profound and perfect, a power of intuition. The lights coming through the gift of understanding quiet the first power, that of reasoning. The soul does not know, it can no longer reason, at least when it is under the influence of the gift of understanding. But now the power of intuition is stimulated more or less consciously by these lights which it receives.

Savor in the will: the gift of wisdom

Finally the gift of wisdom, which is also an antenna, receives a communication from God, a savor which penetrates the will and all the faculties of the soul, producing in them a delightful calm.

In this state the soul is therefore quieted, at times painfully. Let us not think that God's action through the gifts of the Holy Spirit will always be sweet, or that sweetness will predominate. It is possible that there may be suffering. Normally this action of God produces a certain suffering even when there is accompanying sweetness. The paralysis and the suffering are surer signs of God's action than the sweetness we may experience.

However, the intellect is illumined by these lights and the will receives a certain delight. Do not be surprised at these antinomies: the apparent contradiction between suffering and sweetness, paralysis and appeasement. The action of God in the soul is *always* marked by these apparent contradictions. This simultaneous perception of seemingly contradictory things is the surest sign of the authentic action of God.

Attraction to the obscure

Under this action of God, at once pacifying, enlightening and savory, the soul feels itself attracted to obscurity. It perceives nothing, it experiences more than ever the transcendence of God in the darkness. Yet at the same time it feels itself drawn to this darkness, which seems more delightful, desirable and attractive to it than all the clear, distinct lights it could acquire by the simple work of the intellect.

St. Teresa expressed this by saying, "The less I understand, the more I believe and love."[4] The virtue of faith then continues to exercise itself, that is to seek contact with God and to penetrate Him; and it does penetrate Him, impelled by this savor that it finds, and the obscurity, not luminous but savory, which enfolds it. It is more strongly attracted to enter into the divine darkness than into the lights it may receive from time to time.

II — LIVING FAITH, CONTEMPLATIVE FAITH

Faith, thus perfected by the quieting of the lower natural faculties owing to the nourishment served them by the action of God, becomes what is called *living faith*. Joseph of the Holy Spirit, one of the Carmelite theologians who elaborated the now classic theory of these realities, tells us that contemplation — for the exercise of this living faith is what we call contemplation — is nothing else than faith perfected, enhanced, enlightened by the gifts of the Holy Spirit.[5] This living faith which moves toward God is contemplative faith, living faith attracted by the obscurity of God. It remains in contact with this obscurity because all within it is stilled, painfully yet truly.

Contemplation is then the fruit of human activity and divine activity, that is, of the virtue of faith — which is given to us — accompanied and perfected by the activity of God through the gifts of the Holy Spirit. This contemplation is not simply a contact but a union with God, in which there is an exchange. The soul seeks God with all its powers. God gives Himself to the soul, He perfects the activity of its faculties and gives Himself to it.

The perfecting of the faculties

What takes place in this union of contemplation? First there is a perfecting of our faculties. Do not think that the paralysis is a diminution of human activity or, so to speak, a psychic weakness. When I studied these various states of illumination and contemplation with psychiatrists during our congress on psychology, they rightly pointed out to me that these contemplative states are surprisingly similar to certain pathological states. At the level of purely psychological experience there seems to be no difference.

Yet there is this notable difference: the pathological case produces a breakdown, a diminution of the individual, of the activity of the faculties, their powers and fruitfulness, while on the contrary these apparently similar states caused by the action of God produce a development of the faculties' powers together with an increase in the fruitfulness of these souls.

It was this that led some, with a touch of malice, to ascribe the behavior of St. Teresa of Avila to hysteria, and to present her in certain books as hysterical. If we were to compare those states in which she lived for some years with hysteria, we could probably find some resemblances. But we know that the hysterical person eventually breaks down. St. Teresa, on the other hand, after having passed through these mystical states, was acknowledged to be a person possessed of one of the finest minds the world has ever known. Her accomplishments were not merely the fruit of exceptional intelligence but of true genius.

This also explains a St. Thérèse of the Child Jesus. Our review *Carmel* will soon publish the composition books and essays written by Thérèse Martin during the two years preceding her entrance into Carmel, as well as the evaluations we requested from her teachers.[6] Their comments could be summed up in this way: "A pupil like all the others, average in every respect."

And yet this young girl, having received her "Christmas grace,"[7] and then entering Carmel and passing through the stages of contemplation, could a few years later write the beautiful pages we find in *The Story of a Soul*. Some of her writings are admirable from a literary point of view, but we marvel at the spiritual fruitfulness of all of them, and the spiritual revolution which they have launched in the world.

This is the effect of contemplation, of the action of God in the soul which has perfected its natural activity, come to a living faith, achieved union, and thanks to this union, perfected all its faculties.

The transformation of love

As a consequence of this union, an exchange is established with God. God pours forth His grace, transforms the soul, takes it under His rule, and makes it truly His child. The apostle St. Paul, defining the saint and the child of God, says, "All who are led by the Spirit of God are sons of God."[8] The Holy Spirit can, owing to this union brought about with the soul, transmit His light to enlighten it, as well as His motions which will touch the will and direct it.

What is a saint? Not necessarily a person who performs great mortifications, or at least it is not mortifications which make the saint. It is not even the miracles a person can work that make the saint, although they may be an authentic sign of holiness. Sanctity consists in this reign of the Holy Spirit in a soul. He enlightens the soul at each instant, moves it, and makes of it another Christ, another humanity for Christ in which He can do His work and through which He can accomplish His work in the world.

This union of contemplation is a veritable communion. There is the sacramental, Eucharistic communion, in which we receive the body, blood, soul and divinity of Jesus, a communion which operates "*ex opere operato*," that is to say, which necessarily produces as it were its effects in the well disposed soul and nourishes it with supernatural life. There is the communion of obedience: our will is in communion with the will of God and thereby establishes a union, a bond, a communication. Through this union we receive the light, strength and fruitfulness of God. And finally, there is the union of contemplation.

Here it is not solely a prayer. It is an exchange, a descent of God into the soul. Through this a transformation is wrought which is not something extraordinary but which is pointed out by the apostle

St. Paul as something possible for all souls, for every Christian. We contemplate the beauty of God and through this contemplation "we are being changed into His likeness from one degree of glory to another, for this comes from the Lord who is the Spirit."[9] This contemplation achieves sanctity in us. This is its effect.

Collaboration with the Holy Spirit

In prayer, then, we should not merely seek God's help for the various intentions we have, or even the light we need for some given circumstance or project to be carried out. We should primarily seek union, an intimate communication with Him, which allows God to transform us from glory to glory in His likeness.

Union places us under God's rule. The Holy Spirit, who was given to us in baptism and again in a special way on the day of our confirmation, becomes truly the Master of our soul and reigns there through the light with which He illumines our intellect and the impulses whereby He moves our will. He intervenes directly in our life, and this not only momentarily but habitually. He leads us as He wills, and causes us to carry out His will.

Christian apostles who want to do God's work in the world should of course offer Him their persons and activities, together with their resources and everything superfluous they can dispose of. But if they want to be God's collaborators in the building up of the Church, in the salvation of souls, they must place themselves under God's rule, under the rule of the Holy Spirit who is the soul of the Church, the designer of the Church, the one who builds the Church.

This Spirit requires our activity and the cooperation of our intellect and will, but before all else He requires that we respect His rights. He wishes always to be the chief architect Himself, the chief worker. He wills and desires that we be truly collaborators and collaborators only in His work, which is the only fruitful work.

III — THE SPIRIT LIVES IN OUR SOULS

Perhaps when you hear me expounding these marvels — and they are not extraordinary — you may think that they are reserved only for certain souls, saints, and that this kind of contemplation cannot be practiced by most Christians. Allow me a few remarks on the subject before closing.

All are called

Some years ago there was considerable discussion in spiritual reviews about the call to contemplation. Many authors seemed to be saying that contemplation is reserved only for certain chosen souls. The general opinion today, and it is spreading more and more widely because it has been verified by experience, is that contemplation, the contemplative gifts — in other words the action of God in souls, God perfecting our prayer and the natural activity of our powers in prayer — is in fact very frequent.

A fairly broad experience in varying situations gives me the right, I believe, to affirm that these contemplative gifts, this action of God in souls, is at present very widespread. It is not for me to dispute the opinions which held sway in former times. I was not there. I can only speak of what I see at the present time, and I appeal to your own experience.

The gifts of God, the contemplative gifts, are very prevalent. Just now, as you heard me speaking of the quieting experience frequently observed in prayer, of the sense of delightful obscurity found in it, I think that memories must have come to many of you of similar graces you have received. It is not a question here of anything extraordinary such as visions, ecstasies or levitation. It is simply a matter of impressions of recollection you may have experienced at one time or another, or that you habitually experience.

I am convinced that many of you, perhaps frequently or habitually, when entering a church, making an attentive genuflection, looking at the tabernacle, opening your missal at the beginning of Mass, or taking up a book of meditation, have experienced this quieting and felt the need to stop and look at the tabernacle. What were you doing at the time? Nothing, apparently, unless perhaps simply savoring this impression, an impression which did not linger, which you may have had to nourish with prayer or a glance at the tabernacle. But still it was an impression which you did experience.

This impression is normally produced by the gifts of the Holy Spirit. We do not attribute it to exterior circumstances for the simple reason that it does not always occur when the same circumstances are repeated. But this impression — as I call it — is truly the fruit of the gifts of the Holy Spirit. The soul pays little attention to it, does not think it supernatural, and for that reason neglects it.

It seems to me that contemplative gifts are not developed in the soul precisely because they are ignored, not appreciated at their true value, and the means are not taken to develop them. Referring to this St. Teresa says, "God calls everyone."[10] God manifests His call by the graces which He gives on occasion, graces of recollection, the lights or the sense of joy we may feel on a feast day, our First Communion day or after some particularly fervent communion or prayer; in short, whenever He wills. But He does not renew His grace, He does not develop it if the soul does not respond by conduct appropriate to such graces.

At such times there are certain steps to be taken. It is not a question of changing our circumstances or undertaking extraordinary mortifications. It is a question of taking the means precisely suited to God's graces, such as silence and the calming of our activities. Various means are described in spiritual books. It is, too, a question of making sufficient time for prayer in our life, time for the grace of God to blossom and take possession of us. Here we have a true mystical ascesis,[11] which we need to understand and practice.

An overflowing Mercy

This call to contemplation seems to me therefore to be a general one. I dare not say universal, for some souls neither hear nor perceive it; but it is a general call. Allow me to repeat what I said just now. In our day contemplative graces are very numerous, very frequent. To what do we owe this fact? Perhaps to the invasion of evil.

When we consider our world today, we see

that the powers of evil are manifesting a frightening activity. In the Far East especially, we see new conquests in the spread of atheistic communism, and we could well fear for the future if we did not know that our Church is divine and is sustained by the Holy Spirit. And the Holy Spirit reacts against this invasion of evil by spreading His light and grace. God's revenge is always the revenge of mercy. In our Western world as in the Far East — we know from what has been written about Shanghai[12] — the action of God, the action of the Holy Spirit, is truly wondrous.

Yes, this action is wondrous, and we must not neglect grace. When Christ came to Palestine, the Jews, who were actually expecting Him and who had been chosen to await His Kingdom and prepare for it, did not recognize Him. They were looking for something else. Let us hope this will not happen to us, that we will not find ourselves unprepared when Christ returns, when the Spirit of God manifests Himself in souls. Let us hope we shall not be looking for something else, some temporal, perhaps political triumph answering to our own tastes and ideas.

Yes, the Holy Spirit *lives* in our souls, the Holy Spirit *lives* in the world and manifests His life. He manifests it through His grace, through the hold He has on us with His call to each of our souls. And this hold of God which we feel and have sometimes experienced, which is felt by the generality of Christian people, produces a yearning, an unrest. Many souls seek the means of responding to this call of God, of cultivating this grace which they feel and experience at least obscurely. They seek methods, instruction on how to develop this grace and to journey toward those regions to which they feel obscurely called.

I shall try to clarify this doctrine, to explain what we ought to do in order to develop the grace we have been given.

In order to throw practical light on this teaching, we shall turn to our Master, to Jesus, who came into our world to bring us heaven's light and to shed it on our path through this world. We shall consider Christ in His contemplation, so that we may learn to pray and contemplate as He did, that is, to follow in His way, to reach the regions where He would lead us, and attain to that supreme contemplation within the Holy Trinity.

Notes

[1] On analogous language, see "Prayer as Contact with God," 59.

[2] Cf. "Baptismal Grace," 41ff.

[3] Cf. *Summa theologica*, Ia IIae, q. 86.

[4] Cf. *Relations*, 22 Sept., 1572, 29, 334-335.

[5] Cf. Father Marie-Eugene, *I Want to See God*, vol. 1, 341-342.

[6] Cf. *"Devoirs de style et narrations de Thérèse Martin"* ["Compositions and exercises of Thérèse Martin"], *Carmel*, April-May-June 1951, II, 81-107.

[7] Cf. Thérèse's own account, *Manuscript A*, 44 v° and f.

[8] Rm 8:14.

[9] 2 Cor 3:18.

[10] Cf. St. Teresa of Avila, *The Way of Perfection*, ch. 19, 113.

[11] Mystical ascesis, that is, "adapted to the action of God through the gifts" (*I Want to See God*, vol. 1, 360); or "how the soul should behave to prepare for and respond to the action of God" (vol. 2, 74). See more detailed explanation in *I Want to See God*, vol. 1, 356-360 and vol. 2, 72ff.

[12] An allusion to the book *Les enfants dans la ville* [*The Children in the City*] by J. Lefeuvre, from the series *Église vivante* [*The Living Church*], Casterman, Tournai-Paris 1957 (1st ed. 1954), a record of the heroic resistance of Catholic students at Aurora University in Shanghai (1952-1955), to violent communist persecution.

Daily Prayer

This chapter, entitled "Daily Prayer," is not actually a conference, but rather a dialogue in which Father Marie-Eugene responds to the difficulties and questions of his audience. It seems to us that this concrete aspect of the practice of prayer may be very helpful for all who desire to persevere in it.

I shall begin by giving a short summary of some of the difficulties experienced in prayer, and will answer each briefly. Then I shall be happy to discuss these difficulties in a practical way.

To find the time

Regarding prayer, the first difficulty is to find the time for it. This is the initial objection raised by those to whom this spiritual exercise is proposed:

"But I don't have time, I don't have time for silent prayer."

People give excuses. They say:

"We already have our exercises of piety, Sunday Mass, morning and night prayers."

According to the degree of their piety or the form it takes, they may add to this list daily Mass, Communion and a few other things. Then they say:

"We haven't time to do more than this."

All this is obviously true.

"I am the mother of a family. I have my children,"

or on the other hand,

"I have my business, my work, and I don't see how I can fit prayer into my life the way it is set up now. How can I find the time for silent prayer?"

It is certain that, if you want to fit prayer into your life, there is the initial problem of organizing your personal life. To include the exercise of prayer, which may mean anywhere from a half-hour to two hours, in a life that is already organized, seems like an insoluble problem, because we are all busy, overworked, pressured people. Someone may say,

"If I spend an hour in prayer, or a half hour, I will simply be increasing my workload and may become unfaithful to the essential duties in my life, duties to my family, my profession, or my country."

I believe that when a person wants to make room for silent prayer in his life, he must face the problem of organizing his life. Does this mean that he must change his profession, abandon his ordinary occupations, or neglect the duties of his state in life for the sake of prayer? No, I don't think so. Experience proves that very busy people have found time to practice prayer. It is said that from the day that St. Francis Borgia, one of the first Generals of the Society of Jesus, was made General, he increased his time for prayer, and instead of spending three hours, I believe he devoted six hours to it every day. I know other busy people who manage to spend one or two hours a day in prayer.

Let us not be frightened by these two hours of silent prayer. We have only to remember that there are twenty-four hours in the day. Of these twenty-four, we spend eight, perhaps nine, sleeping. That leaves sixteen. I do not know what kind of work you do, but an eight-hour workday is normal for our times. So there are still eight hours left. Out of that, two hours might easily be set aside.

Prayer should not be seen as an accessory. It should be included in our lives as an activity we esteem, as essential as our sleep or rest. At the least, it should be viewed as a very productive practice.

I believe that when organizing our lives we need to be convinced of the usefulness of silent prayer. Most of the time it is omitted because we think of it as a secondary exercise of piety, one we can easily dispense with. We believe we can get to heaven without spending two hours in prayer every day. This may indeed be true, but the point is that we are not really convinced that prayer is a necessary exercise.

What we primarily fail to see is that silent prayer, when included in our lives, brings with it an element of balance. An hour of prayer may not add an hour of complete repose or of sleep to our day, but it certainly adds an hour of balance.

It is often said — St. Francis de Sales in particular says it — that contemplatives act with much greater speed and efficiency than other people. Prayer gives them a period of repose and relaxation and fine tunes their faculties, perfecting them even from a human point of view. In a word, it insures balance. The time apparently "lost" in praying is retrieved through the ability for intense work which it gives us.

To resolve this problem of fitting silent prayer into our lives, we have to take various circumstances into consideration: the quality of our spiritual life, our aptitudes, and the kind of prayer we want to engage in. To spend two hours might seem arduous to some, and would be. Others might think an hour very long, still others, a half hour. But it seems to me that if you want prayer to have some effect on your life, at least a half hour a day is needed.

How to organize the time? A person might divide the time in half, in thirds, or in quarters, depending upon aptitudes, and resolve the problem in this way. I myself have known many busy people, mothers of families, home makers, religious with absorbing duties, preoccupied with government or burdened with heavy correspondence, who manage to spend two or three hours daily in prayer.

When St. Teresa speaks in the First Mansion of including prayer in one's life, she immediately mentions regularity.[1] This is not to say that we have to organize every detail of our existence, but there should be a general organization of life and a fixed hour, a special time set aside for prayer.

Prayer and work

"Can I pray while I am working?"

"Doesn't manual work take away from the depth of my prayer?"

No, quite the contrary. It is a recognized fact that manual labor is particularly favorable to contemplation. It leaves the mind free and consequently enables us to give ourselves to prayer. Contemplatives far prefer manual labor to intellectual work because the latter, engaging the mind, does not allow the same attention to God. We can pray, then, during manual work.

I do not think, however, that we should be content with praying only while we are working. There should be a time for the exercise of prayer outside of work time, and we should give ourselves to it exclusively. Even manual work absorbs a part of our attention and consequently does not allow us to give to God, to prayer, to meditation, all the time and attention they require. From time to time we meet people who say,

"As for me, I think about God all day long, at least very often. I don't need to make a special exercise of prayer."

To these I would say, "No, I believe the exercise is necessary. If you are already thinking of God so easily now, think how much more you will profit by giving God a special time for prayer."

Recollection

During our prayer itself, another difficulty surfaces. Silent prayer requires recollection. It implies attention to God and the focussing of all our faculties on Him. Prayer is an affectionate exchange with God, and from our side this exchange requires that we bring all our faculties to bear on it. We saw this when we were speaking of man's active contribution in prayer, the orientation of his intellect and senses to God. In order to be recollected we need a setting, and particular circumstances. Often enough, a second objection is raised in this connection:

"I cannot recollect myself. I cannot gather my powers together. Or at least, if I manage to control them for a short time, they very soon get dissipated and scatter in all directions."

Difficulty in being recollected, especially for

beginners (later, it takes another form), can best be met by a certain kind of organization, that is, the choice of a *time* and *place* for prayer. St. Teresa insisted strongly on this.

Choosing the time

We have to take into account the fact that silent prayer, especially in its beginnings, calls for the attention of all our faculties. We could call it a rather intense intellectual work. All of us who have given ourselves to intellectual work are well aware that there are some times of the day when we can function more intensely than at others. Some of us are morning people, some are night people. Some can become recollected better in the morning, and others at night.

St. Teresa says that if a person experiences difficulty in being recollected during prayer, the first thing to do is to experiment with a change in the time set aside for prayer. Try it at a different time, to see if it goes better. There is no general rule for this. Each of us has his or her own temperament and aptitudes.[2]

Choosing the place

Different religious Orders, according to the form their contemplation takes, choose different places for their prayer. Cistercians choose valleys, as at Senanque. Most Trappists will be found in valleys too. Benedictines often settle on mountains. Carmelites seek the desert, either in mountains or valleys depending on their situation. Carthusians pay no attention to climate; they settle on mountains, and everything in their location is geared to prayer.

The setting of prayer is very important. You do not find the same style of architecture among Cistercians and Benedictines. Most Benedictine abbeys are built in Gothic style, while Cistercians prefer the Romanesque. It is not a matter of the founder's taste. It stems from a certain harmony between their prayer and its setting. Why do Benedictines choose the Gothic style? Because they seek the splendor of worship, and Gothic or flamboyant Byzantine styles of architecture lend themselves more to this.

Trappist Cistercians, on the other hand, need the beauty of nature and they prefer a Romanesque style, something more austere, more humbling. Carmelites, who seek the desert, want the *nada*, the "nothing," of St. John of the Cross, in order to find the "all" of God. Like St. John of the Cross, they require a certain splendor in their setting, and austerity. But when they build for themselves, they want absolutely nothing that could hold them back from God. For while they make use of sensible things to go to God, they insist on the sensible itself being despoiled, so that it may not hold them back.

These things are of considerable importance. You will say to me,

"But we cannot build a Gothic church at home, or a hermitage in our garden!"

I am merely suggesting that you do not overlook the importance of the place of your prayer. What setting should you choose? That depends upon each one. The setting should be whatever best helps us to be recollected, a place where we are master of ourselves, and not the victim of edginess; a place where we have most control over ourselves and our faculties.

Some people can be very recollected before the Blessed Sacrament. Others, on the contrary, cannot, because as soon as they start to pray they become self-conscious, especially if it is a large church open to the public. They fear being seen by others. You will say to me, "But they ought to overcome that!" But no, we can't always overcome all our feelings. People like this will never be able to become recollected in church.

Is it better to be recollected before the Blessed Sacrament or to seek solitude? Some prefer to pray before the Blessed Sacrament, because they experience a quieting influence there. However, the more general tendency will be not to make one's prayer before the Blessed Sacrament, because there one is exposed to the crowd and does not have the sense of solitude which is necessary for stillness of soul. Each of us, depending on the circumstances of our ordinary life, can choose the most favorable, accessible setting.

To know one's temperament

On the subject of recollection, someone may say,

"But I am fidgety, I'm a nervous person."

Modern doctors, psychiatrists and psychoanalysts, tell us we are all a bit sick. This is not to say, obviously, that we all belong in institutions, but it is certain that we all have one or another leaning. Most of the time this tendency, which is clearly not pathological or apt to produce any real imbalance, affects some one of our powers, our thinking perhaps. Then we may suffer a bit of anxiety....

The tendency to anxiety or melancholy will show up in our prayer and produce a certain disturbance. It is well to be aware of this. There are techniques for handling it. We can use those which have been suggested to us. The technique of breathing, for example, of respiration, can produce real relaxation. I am not saying that it will completely do away with our nervous tension, but it can help a great deal. There are other means besides this.

I think we should not exaggerate in this area,

but there is no law against helping ourselves, at this level, by using techniques which simply relax our anatomy, our physiology. Let us make use of whatever is good in them, but not think that we can achieve true prayer, above all supernatural contemplation, by means of purely natural techniques.

In this matter, we can seek counsel which will be helpful in various circumstances. Furthermore, in most cases these tendencies are minimal. It is simply a good thing to recognize them for what they are. Then we ourselves can compensate for them. If, for example, we are worried, and somewhat inclined to scruples, we might say to ourselves, "Forget it!" Just by ignoring it, we can shake it off. Practically speaking, we will be relieved by ignoring it. A person may be inclined to melancholy, but can make good progress just the same. It is with this as with so many things. We manage to live well in spite of some chronic indisposition or other. It doesn't necessarily prevent us from doing our ordinary work.

These different pathological tendencies of ours are almost sure to come to light, it seems, as we advance in prayer. When our prayer becomes passive and God is acting upon the soul, they surface.

St. John of the Cross compares these tendencies to minerals placed in a hot furnace. As they melt, cinders and clinkers come to the surface.[3] The cinders are not just sins of our past life. Rather, and especially, they are various tendencies. We see them more clearly and take note of them. Moreover, the soul is now moving into unfamiliar terrain, and this normally precipitates, not so much an unleashing of the tendencies, as their stronger influence on our psychological life.

At this point we will clearly need appropriate counsel. The great remedy is awareness of these tendencies. We need to see them. Once they are seen and accepted, a person is already half way to a cure. For what makes a tendency harmful is precisely the fact that we are not aware that it is there and at work within us.

Therefore as the soul progresses in contemplation this problem of recollection can be a delicate one. In the beginning it is enough to take some precautions and to choose a setting. There is no doubt we will receive God's special help.

Liturgical prayer and silent prayer

Another problem is posed in regard to praying interiorly during vocal and liturgical prayer. St. Teresa takes a very definite stand on this. It is safe to say that the Church's current position is an elucidation of all the teaching to be found in St. Teresa. That is to say, we should not be liturgists to the point of believing that the liturgy by itself suffices; and on the other hand, we should not wish to devote ourselves exclusively to purely personal prayer, but should give ourselves to liturgical prayer as well, since it is, properly speaking, the prayer of Christ and of the mystical Body.

We should engage, then, in both liturgical and private prayer. St. Teresa tells us as much. We discover in her, both in her theoretical teaching and in the practical teaching conveyed through her life, this simultaneously liturgical and interior movement. At the monastery of the Incarnation where she lived in her apartments she had a little oratory, and there she solemnly celebrated the feasts of the saints to whom she had special devotion.[4] She honored them by personal as well as liturgical prayer. And on the other hand, she says very clearly that she does not see how liturgical, vocal prayer, can fail to be accompanied by mental prayer.[5] For if we pay no attention to what we are saying, if we are not fully aware that we are speaking to God, our prayer is not even human; it is purely material and external. Consequently we need to think about what we are saying and unite ourselves to the Church when we participate in liturgical prayer.

Such is the proper association of the two. Prayer can be at once mental and vocal, personal and liturgical. This does not prevent our giving to our liturgical prayer, when accompanied by singing, all the attention necessary to make it harmonious.

Activity in prayer

Here is another problem, another difficulty:

"What is silent prayer? How do I pray? Of what does silent prayer consist?"

I believe I have answered this in previous discussions. However, let me sum up and insist on certain points, and above all refute, not so much objections, as false opinions sometimes held regarding prayer.

Meditation and silent prayer

In France in the seventeenth century there was a spiritual renewal which did a great deal of good. Bremond, the author of the book *Sentiment religieux* [*Religious sentiment*][6] speaks of "a mystical invasion" at the beginning of the seventeenth century. When we study history we notice that this mystical invasion was precipitated particularly by the translation of the works of St. Teresa.

The movement was disseminated widely among the clergy by Father Olier, Father de Condren, and St. Vincent de Paul. It then took on a French character, typical of the century, and did it well: a spirituality should be practical and consequently should adapt itself to different kinds of temperaments. And it took on a reasonable form. There followed the celebrated discussion between Fenelon and Bossuet.

Bossuet, with his emphasis on reason, represented the Great Age of the classics. Fenelon on the other hand represented a more affective, perhaps more mystical tendency. It was Bossuet who prevailed in the seventeenth century. Bremond seems to say, as I do myself, that this is somewhat regrettable.

It is obvious that Fenelon may have allowed himself to be unduly influenced by Madame Guyon, but even so, his position may have been closer to the truth than Bossuet's in this matter. However it may be, spirituality became reasonable and intellectual. And it has been transmitted to us in this form, adapted thus to our spirit, passed on, expressed, and accounted for by the spirit of the Great Age.

It so happens that we have preserved — I say we, for it is above all the clergy, formed in the seminaries with the methods of St. Francis de Sales, Olier and the French School — we have preserved those forms of prayer which are predominantly intellectual or meditative. As a result of this our French thought identifies prayer with meditation. What is prayer for us who are French? It is meditation. This is an error.

St. Teresa insisted strongly on this point. When she speaks of the prayer form called meditation or consideration, a basically intellectual activity, she says that it is a good beginning for intellectuals, but that intellectuals need to be reminded — she did not know that her teaching would take this form in

France, because she was already dead when the French School began — they need to be reminded that prayer does not consist in *thinking* but in *loving*.[7]

We need to remember this word of St. Teresa. Prayer is not a meditation but a contact with God, an exchange with God. I think I have insisted on this point. It is the underlying concept which must be guarded and retained. Why do we pray? In order to find God, to have a conversation with Him. How do we make this contact? I am only repeating what has already been said: we make it through faith, through the exercise of theological faith: "My God, I believe you are there and I love you."

Now, we must maintain and nourish this act of faith and love which leads to contact and an exchange with God. How will we nourish it? If we are intellectuals, we can make use of meditation. But we must be careful. Let us not compose philosophical dissertations, or even theological ones, during prayer, because that is not what prayer is. Let us not think we have made an excellent prayer after making a meditation, because we have found many beautiful thoughts and constructed fine syllogisms. If that is all we do, we are not praying.

Ways to make contact with God

The point is to make contact with God. If we are intellectuals we will make it through meditation.

If we are not, we may take a picture, as St. Teresa suggests, and look at it. This is what St. Thérèse of the Child Jesus did. She had a picture she liked, showing a tabernacle with a grille, and she said, "He is the divine Prisoner!"[8] It does not matter! The point is to use what will lead us to contact with God.

Others will use vocal prayer. St. Teresa of Avila recounts: "A person told me she did not know how to pray, that she could not get beyond the words 'Our Father.' But I perceived that with her 'Our Father' she had reached a very high state of contemplation."[9] I myself can tell you of an experience I had in one of our monasteries.

There was a certain nun who had been a Portress for forty-two years in a mountainous city in the center of France. She was hard-working, but did not seem contemplative. She could be seen running back and forth with her basket, and she carried out the duties of her charge admirably. She said to me one day at the end of her life, "Father, I cannot meditate. I am very sad because I cannot pray any longer."

— "What do you do, Sister?"

— "I cannot even say the 'Our Father.'"

— "How do you go about it? Do you try?"

— "Oh yes, I try so often. But when I start, I say 'Our Father' and when I've said that I can't go any further. It is so beautiful that right away... sometimes I close my eyes and force myself. I say, 'Our

Father who art in heaven, hallowed be thy Name….' I can never get beyond that. You see, I am unable to pray."

I am sure that this Sister, on saying "Our Father," plunged into the heart of the Blessed Trinity. I hastened to tell the Prioress, "If you want a mini-course in contemplation, ask your little Portress what she does." See the contact with God, made through contemplation!

There are other methods you can use. Good old people who have worked hard recite their rosary. If you were to ask them,

— "What are you doing?"

— "I'm reciting my rosary."

— "Do you pay attention to the words you are saying?"

— "Oh! No."

But since they lead an active life, their faculties need a certain activity, otherwise they would be restless. One calms oneself as best one can. They calm themselves, and as they murmur their "Our Father" and "Hail Mary" they think of God, of the mystery; and they reach contemplation. Is this a bad way? It is an excellent way.

We each find our own way of making contact with God and maintaining it. Moreover, we can vary it. When St. Thérèse of the Child Jesus was ill, someone who came into her cell asked her,

— "What are you doing?"

— "I'm praying."
— "And what do you say?"
— "Nothing."[10]

She had made contact. That is prayer. We should therefore be convinced about what the essence of prayer truly is. It is making contact with God in order to be enriched by Him, to establish communication with Him through faith, by an act of love.

God's intention is that we should lay hold of what He is, and that He himself should communicate with us and give us, even in a way we do not feel, what He has, that is, His grace. But we need to know for certain that this is not the same thing as meditation. Furthermore, the books on meditation which enjoyed great success thirty years ago are now somewhat out of date. We have come to this concept of a living exchange with God, which we maintain by the means within our power, means which suit our temperament or our dispositions at the time.

You see, therefore, that our prayer in the morning will not be the same as our prayer in the evening. St. Thérèse of the Child Jesus recounts that there was a nun in choir who always rattled her rosary beads and sighed during her prayer. What did Thérèse do? She said to herself, "There's no possibility of being recollected near this Sister. What am I going to do? I will enjoy listening to this annoying noise, and offer it to God."[11] The obstacle became a means of finding God, and she certainly made an excellent prayer. We can make use of everything, on condition that we do not have preconceived incorrect notions about prayer.

Obviously it is necessary to make some preparation for this kind of prayer, a short reading, attentiveness, recollection. We also need to know what we are about to do: to look at our Lord, to read the Gospel or some other book, to say some vocal prayer from time to time. When we are going through a somewhat difficult period of transition, we can ask the advice of an expert, someone who has had some experience in the ways of prayer and who will show us how to proceed. Of course, prayer is an art, a science to be learned. For singing and ceremonies in church, practice is needed. For prayer, which is a far more delicate, synthetic work, requiring the participation of all our faculties, formation is also needed. Appropriate knowledge and counsel are needed.

But there is no condition, even weariness, which dispenses us from prayer or hinders it. Even for persons who at a given moment are suffering from nervous depression or an almost complete lethargy of their faculties, there is the act of faith. St. Teresa tells us: "I know that by a sheer act of faith I can enter into a relationship with God."[12] We can indeed encounter God in this way and be in contact with Him, and He will respond. The result is a certain peace; and even if the peace is not there, a certain communication with God will have been established.

The example of St. Thérèse of the Child Jesus

Most difficulties in regard to prayer can be overcome easily enough by an understanding of the essence of prayer, by seeing things as they are. We discover this in St. Thérèse of the Child Jesus, especially in her letter to Sr. Mary of the Sacred Heart, a remarkable letter which she wrote in September, 1896. It is the second document[13] in the autobiographical group of documents, and seems the slightest, but it is perhaps the most important from a doctrinal point of view.

Thérèse describes how she prayed during a certain period of dryness. Often she even fell asleep, because she was exhausted and could not help herself. She was there in the fog, she said. There was no consolation, not a single good thought, and yet she always came back to God through an act of faith, an act of love. This was her prayer. It is a way which does not seem at all classical, and which we do not find described in any other school. Yet she herself describes it from her own experience.

This way of praying as described by St. Thérèse is so disconcerting that even great masters say it is not contemplative. Yet, what is meant by being contemplative? It means finding God, looking at God, drawing light from God. Thérèse did this admirably. If it was not through contemplation that she found Him, how else was it? Moreover we discern in her, even in this description, a gaze of her soul which carries her immediately toward God, brings her to God.

She herself said that she never spent more than three minutes without thinking of God.[14] What is this look at God? Clearly it is contemplation. St. Thomas tells us that contemplation is a simple gaze on God. She had this. She was, therefore, truly a contemplative. Contemplation does not consist in extraordinary graces, ecstasies, and experiences of God. It is the gaze itself. I believe it is very important for us to pay attention to this definition, in order to pray ourselves.

There is no point in protesting that we have no education, no learning, etc. Obviously, we need to know something of the catechism, we need to read the Gospels and be nourished gradually by spiritual reading, if we are to pray. But it is not necessary to be a great theologian or an intellectual. Lofty theology is not as closely connected with true contemplation as is purely affective prayer.

It is rather astounding. We would be inclined to think that a great theologian, who lives with dogmas and is accustomed to study and scrutinize them, would have greater facility in praying. In reality he still has a long way to go, and he may meet with obstacles that hinder him considerably. As a result he may find himself further from true supernatural contemplation than the simple soul who lacks extensive theological knowledge but knows the catechism and loves God. This is not intended as a disparagement of study. By no means. We must study, we must attain knowledge, we must have a foundation for our faith and our prayer. But we do not have to be advanced theologians.[15]

The problem of feeling

"If a person does not truly feel an intense love of God within him, how can he know when he loves God?"

You do not have to know it, you have only to do it. Faith does not consist in feeling. We have here a more difficult problem, that of feeling and experience. At the level of faith and love, feeling is something accessory, even though many people today, especially our modern authors, are convinced of the opposite.

A spiritual movement began at the beginning of this century with great converts like Peguy, Claudel, Jacques Riviere, Psichari. These conversions came about for the most part after an emotional experience. Claudel was converted at Notre-

Dame during the singing of the *Magnificat* on Christmas Day. He *felt it*. For Jacques Riviere it was somewhat the same thing and he gives us a definition of faith which is false, even though it is he who gives it: "Faith," he says, "is a bird one feels in the night."[16] This may not be an exact quotation but that is the sense of it. So anyone who feels the touch of a bird has faith; otherwise, not. This is a theological error.

Faith is an act of adherence to God, an act of the virtue of faith: "My God, I believe." Do I feel anything? No. A feeling accompanying this is something accessory; the light which may be given in some cases is accessory. The act of faith is an adherence, it is the submission of my intellect, an allegiance through the virtue of faith, that faculty which was given to me in baptism, and by which I say, "I believe."

This virtue is able to bridge the distance separating me from God and to penetrate Him. When I have penetrated Him, do I have more light? I have the light of the truth which has been given to me in a dogmatic formula, such as, for example, "My God, I believe in you, in your existence; I believe that there are three Persons in you." But does this mean that I have an experience, a feeling of light? Not necessarily. In any case, the experience of light which I may have does not indicate anything about the quality of my faith.

Let us take the example of St. Thérèse of the Child Jesus. At the end of her life, God knows whether she had faith, hope and charity. She had reached the highest degree of the spiritual life, and yet she could hardly bear to think of God in this sense, that each time she made an act of faith, she felt as if she were adhering to nothing.[17] It was her great anguish, all the more intense because throughout her entire life, whenever she had thought of heaven and God she had enjoyed a sensible feeling. It had been enough for her to think of heaven to be consoled. And now at the end of her life, she found only anguish in the thought and feared she might blaspheme. At this point she had perfect faith, a faith of adherence all the more perfect since she felt nothing.

This is difficult to understand. However, it is the truth. The object of faith is obscure. So let us not confuse faith with light. This is perhaps one of the tendencies, one of the errors, of the nineteenth century. Thinkers constructed an apologetics of light. They wanted to convince people that everything was very reasonable and clear. Unfortunately, they succeeded in making atheists. In teaching catechism to children we must obviously give them the truth — dogma — and tell them all that we are able to know and understand about God. But I believe the essential thing is to give them a sense of mystery, of the infinite.

Perhaps the apologetics of the nineteenth century — this is just my personal opinion, I could be mistaken, perhaps I should even like to be a bit mistaken — this apologetics of reason and clarity has led us to a kind of atheism. For if we are convinced that faith is the same as clarity or light, if we tell that to a child, then when he is nineteen he will re-think his faith. At this point, discovering the truth, he will say: "But they were telling me fairy tales; none of it is true." I am not speaking only of Santa Claus, I am speaking of other truths which will now be for him nothing more than symbols. When he is no longer moved by the credulity of a child who willingly accepts whatever is told him, but rather by passions which lead him to become far more demanding and almost to deny dogmas if he can, he will say, "I no longer have faith."

If, on the other hand, you form him to mystery, saying to him: "My friend, I am not going to explain God to you; God is infinite," the child has a sense of mystery. Now we know something about this mystery: how do we adhere to it? My young friend, we adhere with our will. I prove that I must adhere, but that in adhering, I do not understand.

"I understand as far as faith goes, but what about love?"

The supernatural love which is given to us in baptism is not a sensate love. Why do you want it to be felt? We cannot change values, we cannot catch

Hertzian waves with a workman's spade! Use the proper instrument. If I tell a workman to go and gather up with his spade the Hertzian waves which are passing through the streets, will I then say they do not exist because he is unable to catch them?

Supernatural love is not sensible love. Do not say that it does not exist because you cannot grasp it with your senses. It has another nature. Love is something we shall grasp in heaven, when we shall have glasses adapted to it, that is, the *lumen gloriae*, the light of glory. In this world all we have is dark glasses. Faith gives us dark glasses, or as St. John of the Cross says,[18] it blinds us. We have the eyes of owls staring at the sun. So the more we look, the more we weep, the less we understand. St. Teresa tells us: "The less I understand, the more I believe, and the more I love."[19] "The more she loves" does not mean "the more she feels."

The supernatural world which is opened up to us in baptism is not a matter of refreshing water or fire which we can feel. It is a reality to which we adhere by faith, and faith does not give explanations. St. John of the Cross tells us that the highest knowledge we can have of God is to know that we cannot know Him.[20]

Our life of prayer will be based on this obscurity. Do you know who experienced the obscurity of God most deeply? It was the Blessed Virgin. She lived most fully in the mystery of God because she had advanced further than any other human person. The deeper we plunge in, the less we see. At the same time, the Blessed Virgin had the most light. In the supernatural world there are antinomies, contradictions, light and darkness. Imagine a soul who enjoys extraordinary graces. If she explains everything she has seen, and if she does not have a sense of obscurity and of the infinite, do not believe her. She has made it up. For she has not touched God, she has not touched the infinite. She has not experienced the infinite if she does not have a sense of obscurity and a conviction that the supernatural is beyond her reach.

We should take into account this essential notion of prayer: the supernatural is beyond us. "I have never made so many acts of faith and love," St. Thérèse of the Child Jesus tells us.[21] She had written the *Creed* with her blood and carried it on her person, and to simplify the "act," she simply touched the paper.[22] Consider this act of faith. She had never been in such darkness.

A direct testimony

Allow me to tell a story which goes back about twenty years. It is about a religious who before entering Carmel had been the directress of a boarding school. She was an absolutely remarkable person. Yet she had lived through such states of dryness and obscurity that she could not even pronounce the name of God without experiencing frightful obscurity, a terrible darkness. This lasted for about twenty or thirty long years.

She had described her state to great theologians who told her that St. John of the Cross speaks of twelve or fifteen years spent in this condition, but never much longer. I myself was consulted at one point. I said to myself, "When I do not understand, there is nothing to do but accept. Here is a very levelheaded, highly intelligent person, who in ordinary life shows great balance and absolutely remarkable virtue. I have to believe that God is working here. It is impossible to understand what is happening, but after all, God is not obliged to explain everything to us."

She was very sensitive, and said to me, "When I die, I beg you not to discuss my state with the community, because it would grieve them too much to know how I have suffered all these years." In order to make an act of faith, she used a formula that had been given to her in which there was no mention of the word "God," because this word caused her such suffering. She was pathological, you will say. How quickly we say, "pathological," when we do not understand. It is a little naive to say that someone is ill. Often enough, it is simply an avowal of our own ignorance. To make a long story short, this was the nun's situation. She said to me, "At the moment when I am dying, how am I going to enter the next world, in this state?" I said to her, "Be at peace, God will take care of everything." And so He did.

I was there myself at the moment of her death. When I reached the room where she lay dying, she said to me, "Father, it is much more beautiful than anything you told me." She had had an experience on the eve of her death. She died the next morning. She said to me: "For thirty years, since I have been in this state of darkness, I have had as it were a sense of obscurity, of night, of a kind of hell, and now at the last moment it has been lifted." She added, "Father, this is why I am telling you this. Tell my story to encourage souls who are in darkness. I asked you before to say nothing, but now I beg you, do make known what has happened to me, so that souls who are in this night may know that there is something beyond it."

This was a soul who had, as it were, almost come back from the other world, and she died in transports of joy. All the suffering, the obscurity, had caused her face to become very pale. She gave the impression of a very peaceful person, but all her features were stamped with suffering. Her whole external bearing revealed a person who had suffered enormously. This soul had to suffer for certain intentions: the Church has need of such sufferings.

On the day of her death, she had the religious come to her one by one, and to each she gave a spiritual bouquet for the future, speaking of heaven as if she were already there. And the religious of Carmel were astonished to hear her speaking in this way. It was so unusual for her.

I tell you this story which I have already told many times because for me it throws light on an entire dogma. One truly feels that the teaching of St. John of the Cross is illustrated by a soul who experienced all this.

We find in other souls the same thing in different forms. I believe that often in monasteries of contemplatives there are souls who are living in a kind of expectancy, because they are already in heaven. They speak of "heaven begun" and use other such beautiful expressions. I can give you my testimony. I have known two hundred, perhaps three hundred monasteries of contemplatives. In all these monasteries there is aridity, night, and the obscurity of faith.

St. Teresa said: "If you find a soul who is always joyous, take care: she must be ill."[23] This seems to contradict the definition of love. However, these nuns are souls who love God. If love were something sensible, they would all rise to the ceiling! No, they live these dogmatic truths, these catechism truths, in simplicity.

This is not theology for intellectuals; it is catechism for all the faithful. St. Thomas tells us[24] that the object of faith, which is God, is essentially obscure. If there is clarity in God, it is a halo, secondary dogmas, dogmatic formulas. But the object of faith is obscure. Therefore, when you enter on the way of prayer, make up your mind to persevere. Persevere in persevering. You will see nothing, and the further you advance the darker it will get!

Antinomies

"But didn't God also say we would be radiant with joy?"

The spiritual life is made up of antinomies, paradoxes, apparent contradictions. St. Thérèse of the Child Jesus said at the end of her life, "Love is all that matters."[25] She loved God, we have to admit it, and yet she said, "Do you see that black hole in the garden? That is an image of my soul." But immediately she added, "I am in amazing peace."[26] The spiritual world is characterized by these antinomies.

Think of our Lord's state in Gethsemane and on Calvary. It was a "mystical," spiritual state. Our Lord enjoyed the beatific vision. He did not cease to be the Man-God, to have the beatific vision, and at the same time He suffered intensely. This is the perfect state. On Calvary it was the same thing: "My Father, why have you abandoned me?"[27] — and at the same time He enjoyed the beatific vision. These are antinomies.

The Church presents the Cross to us as the

ideal, the model of redeemed humanity. We all climb Calvary one way or another. Consequently we will find antinomies. I have spoken of obscurity in these elevated states; I have stressed the obscurity. But I did not say that there was no peace, no growth in this obscurity. However, the growth, the enhancement, is not so complete as to be transformed into light, joy, and exaltation.

What I call "antinomies," these opposite states, are, once more, a sign of the spiritual. Even when a soul goes into ecstasy, or is in a state of exaltation, if this state is not accompanied by the Cross its supernatural origin and reality are suspect. These contrasting states, poles apart, can only be described successively. Suffering and joy cannot be described simultaneously; there must be a space between. But although the awareness of them may be successive, they are lived almost simultaneously.

Here we have been describing some of the most elevated states of the spiritual life. But it is good to do so, since these lofty states throw light on the first steps we take in their direction.

Contemplative prayer is accessible to everyone: God is faithful

"Could the mother of a family lead this kind of prayer life?"

In regard to prayer, we must always remember the great principle: it is contact with God, and it always takes two to accomplish it. For your prayer, God will give you grace adapted to your state.

"If it is not felt, if it calls for an effort of the will?"

I said that it might not be felt, but I did not say that it would be a sin to feel it! I believe that if the mother of a family, who prays and perseveres — and as St. Teresa says, "In prayer we do not succeed by main strength,"[28] we have to use discretion — if this mother needs consolation, needs to feel something, I can assure you in the name of God that she will feel as much as she needs. It is not a matter of asking for the feeling. God will provide it as He sees fit, and He will sustain her.

St. Teresa tells us, "Persevere, persevere! I assure you God will do His part and you will therefore be sustained." Experience shows that, all things considered, success follows without the soul's knowing how, regardless of feeling. After a certain time the soul no longer worries about it since, beyond what St. Teresa calls sensible consolations there is, on the contemplative plane, a higher experience.

In the higher regions the soul experiences a sentiment which, as St. Paul says, surpasses all understanding,[29] not in intensity, but in quality. This experience takes the place of the consolation which we craved in the beginning. It fills the soul and sustains it in a much more remarkable way.

In this connection, I just now spoke of dryness. I was speaking at the time of a state at the sensible and intellectual level, almost inferior. This state is accompanied on the higher plane by a more spiritual experience which always occurs. It is called "knowledge through connaturality," and is given by love. It is no longer intellectual, explicit knowledge properly so called; it is not consolation felt by the senses. This knowledge of connaturality is felt in the depths of the soul and fills it, clearly. Even the nun of whom I was just speaking, who could not hear an expression of dogma without her intellect experiencing torment, felt in the depths of her soul that this torment, this anguish, was good. She must have been sustained by a power and savor which she could not experience at sense level.

There are still other developments on the level of mystical experience, but this is another matter. In any case, God does His part when we do ours. Of course there are dangers, but usually danger arises when a person expects sensible consolation and looks for it. We should go to prayer for the sake of God, to converse with Him. We say to Him: "You know what I am, you know what I want, you know what I need." And once more I repeat, God gives us what we need.

Notes

[1] Cf. St. Teresa of Avila, *The Interior Castle*, 2nd Mansion, 297ff.
[2] Cf. St. Teresa of Avila, *Life*, 84-85.
[3] Cf. St. John of the Cross, *The Dark Night of the Soul*, II, 339.
[4] Cf. *Life*, ch. 6, 53-54.
[5] St. Teresa of Avila, *The Way of Perfection*, ch. 25, 131-132.
[6] Cf. H. Bremond, *Histoire litteraire du sentiment religieux en France*, II, *L'invasion mystique (1590-1620)*, Paris, Bloud et Gay, 1930.
[7] Cf. *The Interior Castle*, 4th Mansion, ch. 1, 867-868.
[8] Cf. *Manuscript A*, 31 v.
[9] Cf. *The Way of Perfection*, ch. 30, 152.
[10] Cf. St. Thérèse of Lisieux, *Last Conversations*, 228.
[11] Cf. *Manuscript C*, 30 re.
[12] Cf. *The Way of Perfection*, ch. 26, 134.
[13] This is in *Manuscript B*.
[14] Cf. Céline Martin (Sr. Genevieve of the Holy Face), *A Memoir of My Sister, St. Thérèse*, 104.
[15] On this whole question, see the two chapters of *I Want to See God*: "Spiritual Reading" (vol. 1, 214-233) and "Theology and Supernatural Contemplation" (vol. 1, 491-517). Father Marie-Eugene writes in particular: "Prayer, especially in its beginnings, has need of revealed truth. It can only establish contact with God through faith. Now if faith only touches God through adherence to a formula of revealed truth, with all the more reason should it be nourished with abundant and varied food in order to assure this habitual contact with God in prayer" (vol. 1, 216-217).
[16] Cf. J. Rivière, *A la trace de Dieu*, Paris, Gallimard, NRF, 1925, 335.
[17] Cf. *Manuscript C*, 5 v° ff.
[18] Cf. St. John of the Cross, *The Ascent of Mount Carmel*, bk. II, ch. 6, 119-120.
[19] *Relation* 29, 335.
[20] Cf. St. John of the Cross, *The Spiritual Canticle*, str. 7, 440.
[21] Cf. *Manuscript C*, 7 r°.
[22] *A Memoir of My Sister, St. Thérèse*, 188.
[23] Cf. *The Interior Castle*, 4th Mansion, 332-334.
[24] Cf. *Summa theologica*, IIa IIae, q. 8.
[25] Cf. *Last Conversations*, 262.
[26] Cf. *Yellow Notebook*, 28/8/3.
[27] Mt 27:46.
[28] Cf. *The Interior Castle*, 302.
[29] Cf. Ph 4:7.

The Perfect Contemplative Prayer of Christ

We shall now consider the perfect contemplative prayer of Christ.

The Our Father

Our Lord prayed much in the course of His public life, and His Apostles, who lived with Him constantly, were aware that He was praying. They saw Him go off to a distance, sometimes during the daytime, frequently at night, and give Himself to prayer, very lengthy prayer. They were evidently quite surprised at this, and one day they hazarded a request: "Master, teach us to pray."[1] And as He generally did during His public life, our Lord answered in a way that was certainly perfect, but at the same time brief. He proclaimed His message, and left His Apostles, and later His Church, to explain it and adapt it to various souls and different generations.

You know Christ's answer. Our Lord said to them: "When you pray, pray thus," and He taught them the Our Father. "Our Father, who art in heaven, hallowed be thy name...." This prayer, the Our Father, gives a summary of all the requests we can make to God, and indicates as well precisely what our attitude should be when we address God.

In the course of the centuries the Church, and great spiritual masters such as St. Augustine, St. Thomas, and St. Teresa of Avila, wishing to teach us about prayer, commented on the Our Father. St. Teresa especially, in her *Way of Perfection*, which is her treatise on prayer, comments on the Our Father and draws from its formulas a complete teaching on prayer and contemplation.[2]

And yet this answer of our Lord's seems rather brief. Jesus was teaching His Apostles vocal prayer, which is the prayer of beginners. It is not however exclusively for beginners. St. Teresa will tell us that it is very good, necessary even, for great contemplatives who have reached the heights of contemplation. Vocal prayer is also the prayer of the masses. But this prayer which is expressed exteriorly by the body and by formulas learned and recited in common, opens up before our eyes almost the entire mystery of the prayer of Christ.

Nowadays, we want something more than the recitation of a formula. We know how to pray vocally. We want to know how Christ prayed interiorly. Nowadays the Church invites us to pray liturgically together with the priest, reciting the Mass formularies and even joining in the Divine Office. But this does not entirely resolve the problem.

I — THE MYSTERY OF THE PERSON OF JESUS

How could Christ pray interiorly? To resolve this problem, we need to enter into the mystery of Christ, which is the hypostatic union.[3] We have tried to study, in our earlier discussions, the human mechanism of prayer: our part, the activity of the senses, of the intellect, of faith, and the coordinated activities of all our energies, energies of our physical and intellectual life and our spiritual life of grace.

In our second conference we studied the activity of God. God not only responds to this contact effected by our supernatural energies, our supernatural faculties or infused virtues, especially the virtue of faith. He also collaborates with our powers, especially with the virtue of faith, through the gifts of the Holy Spirit. He perfects our faith in its exercise, calming our intellectual powers and senses.

In the prayer of Christ there was both human and divine activity. If it is possible for us to study the prayer of Christ as the prayer of a man, and to consider the activity of His human faculties one after another, and then the activity of God upon these faculties, the fact remains that between the activity of the human faculties in Christ and in us there is still only an analogy. And again, there is only an analogy between the activity of God in Christ and in us, because Jesus Christ holds a unique position through the hypostatic union.

A transcendent mystery

We know from our catechism that Jesus is the second Person of the Blessed Trinity, the Word, obviously God. He has a divine nature; He is God. In us there is grace, but this participation in the life of God is a created participation, which remains finite. In Christ there is the divinity itself, therefore infinite. And this infinity is not something external to Him, it is part of Him. The second Person of the Holy Trinity is God.

The apostle St. Paul will say that the divinity in Christ was emptied out, but this emptying out of the divinity in Him is only apparent. The divinity, the second Person of the Blessed Trinity, only renounced the external manifestation of the infinitude within Him. The divinity in itself was in no way diminished. Jesus is God. He is infinite.

At the same time, Christ possessed humanity, a humanity like ours, a complete humanity in which we can distinguish a physical life like ours. Christ had members, sense powers. He had a soul like ours, a human soul. But this human soul, this human nature in Christ, identical with ours, was wholly penetrated by the divinity.

It had its own operations, its human operations, but these are qualified in the catechism and in theology with a special name, because of the union of the human nature with divinity in Christ. Owing to the fact that Christ's human nature did not subsist in itself but in the Person of the Word, its operations were attributed to the Person of the Word. Hence the name given to the operations of Christ's human nature is "theandric."[4] Christ therefore possessed something totally unique. This is an unmitigated mystery for us.

How did the hypostatic union come about? How was this union of the human and divine natures effected? We can hardly conceive it, and religious souls, who are penetrated by the transcendence of God and have a certain perception — if it be true that one can perceive it at all — of the infinity of God, are disconcerted by the hypostatic union, the union of the divine and human natures.

When we read the history of the first centuries of Christianity we see that the faithful at that period were wholly penetrated with the Pauline teaching, that is, with a living doctrine which had nothing formalistic about it but which went to the essence, to the Holy Spirit dwelling in the soul, to the grace which established unity throughout the entire Mystical Body of Christ. These Christians, whose ardent, living faith was frequently, even daily exercised in meditation and the realization of these lofty truths of Christianity, engaged in passionate discussions of the divinity of Christ and His human nature.

The discussions on the reality of Christ's humanity were not limited to controversies among theologians, such as still occur, but they extended to the masses of the Christian people. One of the most successful errors in the first centuries was the denial of Christ's true humanity. Christians were so gripped by the concept of the transcendence of the divinity that only with great difficulty could they comprehend the unity of divinity and humanity in Christ.

The Church has taken a clear stand and affirmed for us the true existence of humanity in Christ, of two natures in Christ, divine and human. Yet it remains a mystery.

Luminous ridges

In the landscape of this mystery of the humanity of Christ, which is the mystery of Christ Himself, we find so to speak luminous veins. Like every mystery, like God Himself, this mystery looks to us like a dark cloud, yet a cloud with a luminous face. It is like the cloud which guided the Hebrews in the desert.[5] There is in the mystery of Christ Jesus not only a luminous face, that of His humanity, gentleness, goodness, His love for humanity, but there are luminous ridges or veins which plunge us into the depths of the infinite and of God.

We are separated from these by a darkness, an obscurity which heaven itself will not entirely dissipate. We shall see more clearly there because we shall have the light of glory, the *lumen gloriae*[6] by which to penetrate this mystery, but there are depths which we shall never plumb completely. St. John of the Cross tells us that in this world the reward of the contemplative arriving at the summit is to discover in the mystery of Christ precisely these luminous ridges — "luminous veins" he calls them — which reveal the richness of the mystery of Christ.[7] These luminous ridges are obviously the affirmations of the existence of the divinity and humanity and at the same time certain privileges of Christ's humanity.

When we enter upon a study of the prayer of Christ, we learn that His intellect was endowed with several forms of knowledge. By His knowledge of intuitive vision Christ already had the *lumen gloriae* in this world and perceived the divinity which was in Him, that divinity which is compared to an unction penetrating both His body and soul profoundly. He enjoyed this vision of the divinity in full light, already, not to an infinite degree, since His humanity was created and therefore finite, but yet

He enjoyed it continually. He contemplated this divinity within Him, since it penetrated Him entirely.

To this knowledge of intuitive vision, in the light of which He beheld the divinity, God Himself, and saw also all created things in God, there was added infused light, that is to say ideas, lights, which God Himself placed in His human intellect. These included all the lights and all the knowledge required for Him to exercise His various functions, and particularly His function as priest and mediator between God and man.

To this infused knowledge was added, finally, an experiential knowledge, a knowledge which Christ acquired through the exercise of His faculties. His intellect, which penetrated God thanks to the intuitive vision of light, still exercised itself and, like every human intellect, discovered new ideas and worked on sense data and on the light which came to Him either from without or from within. Hence it was an experiential knowledge which implied, in Christ, true growth.

When the Gospel tells us that Christ grew in wisdom, age and grace before God and man,[8] this does not mean, as some have rather naively suggested, that He merely allowed the knowledge He already possessed to show. No, this was new experiential knowledge over and above what He already possessed.

People sometimes say: "He possessed all knowledge, and so from time to time He showed men that He knew." They seem to be saying that Jesus Christ played at being a man — that He knew everything, and from time to time manifested it. No, it was not at all like that. He had experiential knowledge, and it increased. The Letter to the Hebrews tells us that He learned obedience through what He suffered.[9] It is clear therefore how this experiential knowledge resembled the knowledge which we acquire.

Thus we see the two extremes, human nature progressing, almost painfully, as in the Letter to the Hebrews, learning by what He suffered; and at the same time a complete knowledge through intuitive vision. How is this latter added? How do the two fit together? This is the mystery. There is no way we are able to understand and resolve the mystery of Christ by our own reasoning.

It is like our knowledge of God Himself. We have to recognize before God that we are finite and He is infinite; that God made many things greater than we, and that it is very good of Him to reveal to us even a little of what takes place in His intimate life and in Christ. We have no right to demand — it would be foolish to do so — that He explain everything to us, since it is all far beyond us. God Himself exceeds us infinitely. But it has pleased Him to reveal enough to enable us to imitate Him.

II — THE PRAYER OF JESUS THE MAN-GOD

After this simple glance at the mystery of Christ, let us try now, with the help of the brief, but I think sufficient, ideas we have formed, to see how Christ prayed.

A prolonged prayer

One truth stands out clearly when we study our Lord: He prayed much. When we consider His life, the life of the Word made flesh, the second Person of the Blessed Trinity, and ponder on how He descended into our world to assume humanity in the womb of the Virgin Mary through the work of the Holy Spirit and became like us, we see that of the nearly thirty-three years He spent among us thirty were spent in Nazareth. Why? So that He might live an ordinary life, the kind of life we live ourselves. We might stress the fact that He was a workman, but I believe we should emphasize above all precisely the hidden setting which He chose.

Let us try to enter into the soul of Christ. He knows that He is charged with a mission. Thanks to His knowledge through intuitive vision, His infused knowledge, He knows that He is a mediator, a priest, and that He has come to bring us a message from God, to tell us what takes place in God. He comes, at the same time, to teach us the way to God, and to institute the sacraments so as to give us the life which is in God and in Himself.

He has not come merely to create a new civilization but truly to bring the life of God into this world and to transmit it effectively through His teaching, His suffering, and His sacraments, especially the sacrament of the Eucharist. Never was there a man with such a mission to fulfill. His mission was not only the establishment of a new order but the overturning of the old — a mission obviously beyond any human power.

Now, to fulfill this mission, what is Christ going to do? What should we have done? We should have been in a great hurry, of course, to get to work. Thirty or thirty-three years would be little enough time to accomplish such a mission. But what does Christ do? For thirty years He remains in solitude. From a purely human viewpoint of external activity, He is wasting time.

Why does He go to Nazareth? In order to carry out His mission as Man-God, His mission of mediator. Let us not say, "Well, He knew He was all powerful, that He had omnipotence at His disposal, and so He said to Himself, 'I can do it all in an instant.'" No, that was not it. All His actions, the very ordering of His life, the organization of His time, a God-given treasure, hold a lesson for us. He spends almost thirty years in Nazareth, because He judges that the most important role He has to fulfill is that of an ordinary, hidden life, which will leave Him free for the primary duty of prayer.

What is the role of Christ? To all appearances He works with His foster father, St. Joseph. Looking below the surface, we perceive that He is carrying out effectively the exercise of union — if we can say that He needs an exercise for this.

What is this prayer of union of Christ's, which He begins at Nazareth and will continue? After having spent nearly thirty years at Nazareth, He will enter upon His public life and will deliver His message over the next three years. Before beginning His public life, he will spend forty days in the desert in prayer.[10] In the course of His public life, from its very beginning, after His first success at Capernaum, He will leave His Apostles and hide Himself during the nights in the desert, on the mountains, to pray.[11] When He wishes to choose His Apostles, He begins by praying.[12]

The evangelists are unanimous on this point. Throughout His entire life, Christ repeatedly retires into solitude to pray. At the end of His life, during the final days, He spends the night in prayer in the Garden of Gethsemane.[13] Judas, planning to betray Him, knows well where to find Him. He has no need to send out spies to see where He, the Christ who knows His Passion is drawing near, is on this night. Judas leads his troop unerringly to the Garden of

Gethsemane, where Jesus is accustomed to pray every evening and to spend His nights.

On Calvary Jesus continues to pray, and the apostle St. Paul tells us that now that He is ascended into heaven, and dies no more, He ever lives to make intercession for us.[14]

We can say, therefore, that the principal function of Christ in this world, to which He has devoted the greater part of His time, whatever His external occupations might be, is clearly prayer.

The perfect prayer of union

What is this prayer of Christ?

In order to understand it, we need first to consider Christ Himself. How is the union of divinity to humanity effected in Him? Contemplation is the union of humanity with divinity. In Christ, divinity penetrates humanity. Humanity itself is plunged into divinity by a very simple gaze, a gaze which is an intuitive knowledge of God, the *lumen gloriae,* the light of glory which we shall enjoy in heaven. The union, then, is perfect: God's penetration into man, and at the same time man's penetration into God, humanity's penetration into God, by the very simple gaze of the intuitive vision.

Thus this prayer of Christ plunges into God. And here, "into God" means not only into the unity of God, but into the intimate life of God in the Blessed Trinity. The Word in Christ contemplates and loves God the Father, the Father loves His Son, and from the two together, from this knowledge, this light, this infinite perfection which they discover in each other, or rather in the divinity which is common to them both, proceeds the Holy Spirit, substantial Love, the third Person of the Blessed Trinity.

There is a scene in the Gospel which gives us a visible picture of this prayer. The evangelists tell us that when Jesus is baptized He is at prayer.[15] At this moment the Holy Spirit descends upon Him in the form of a dove. John the Baptist, on the banks of the Jordan, sees this manifestation of God above Jesus and thus recognizes Him as the Messiah. The Holy Spirit has given him to know that the Messiah is the one over whom He will descend in the form of a dove.[16] And at the same time the Father speaks: "This is my beloved Son in whom I am well pleased."

We have here an outward portrayal of the prayer of Christ. God the Father engenders His Son: "This is my beloved Son." Christ Jesus is the Son of God, and God expresses Himself thus in Christ. At the same time the Holy Spirit descends upon Him, or rather He is in Him, He manifests Himself in the form of a dove. In reality there is a spiration of the Father and a spiration of the Son, which produces the Holy Spirit.

In this spiration Christ Jesus finds a beatitude, a joy which inundates all His powers. The bliss is infinite for His divinity and finite of course for His humanity — for this humanity of Christ, since it is created, is not capable of the infinite.

One day on Tabor our Lord will manifest His prayer to the Apostles by associating them with it.[17] As often happened, Christ begins to pray. The Apostles are near Him. On this occasion He has taken Peter, James, and John with Him, and they, scarcely comprehending the mystery, are asleep. Then they awaken, to enter, so to speak, into the prayer of Christ. There is an outpouring of His divinity into His humanity, and this outpouring, this light, envelops them too. They are covered, the Gospel tells us, in a "luminous cloud,"[18] which is an emanation, a radiation from God pouring into the humanity of Christ. They experience in their senses, in themselves, in their souls, something of the prayer of Christ.

We are told that Peter, inebriated by this radiation of the prayer of Christ which he is experiencing, wishes to build his tent on Tabor. This is what the prayer of Christ is: the shining of the divinity through His humanity; while at the same time His humanity penetrates the divinity with a gaze. It is a perfect union, therefore, the perfect and experienced realization of the hypostatic union in Christ.

We can well understand, now, why Christ spends His nights in prayer. All His faculties, His whole body, rest in this supernatural bath of the divinity which penetrates Him, strengthening and refreshing Him more than physical sleep. Such is the prayer of Christ, the prayer of union.

To share in the life of God

This prayer of union clearly has value in itself. For why did the Word become flesh? To reestablish union. Often when we read the Gospel we linger over details, which of course have their importance; but a detail must not cause us to forget the whole, the end, the principal work, which is the union of humanity with the divinity; the leading of man to God, the bringing of man to his ultimate goal.

We come from God and we are returning to God. Our true vocation, our goal in life, is not only the perfect development of our human nature, accompanied by a spiritual enhancement which would make us children of God but at a distance, and would be designed to insure a certain balance, a certain happiness for our human nature. No! The divine vocation which God has given us, beginning with grace and the divine sonship it assures us, is to return to God.

Our end is not any happiness whatsoever,

which would be the lot of a person who has behaved well and fulfilled the moral law, who has been an honest man, a perfect Christian, even going to Mass. Our vocation, the end which God has assigned for our life, is to return to Him, to the divine life from which we came forth without knowing it, that is, without having experienced it. Our vocation is to return to God, to share in His divine life, to enter into His rhythm and to be united with Him forever.

The immortality of our soul is not the simple immortality of a soul which has developed, enjoys itself, and thanks to its faculties and perfections can attain to a certain enjoyment of God. No, our object, our end, is to enter into God. There are only three Persons in God, the Father, the Son, and the Holy Spirit; but through grace we are God's children. We are identified with the Word incarnate, with Christ Jesus, and it is He who causes us to enter into the rhythm of Trinitarian life and to share in its works, its light, its privileges and its happiness. This is our end: the Blessed Trinity.

Our prayer in this world should be the prayer of union, a prayer of union with Christ who takes us in charge, who wills that we should identify with Him. He gives us His life, His grace, all that He is, and He then asks to take charge of us, He asks that we attach ourselves to Him. At the moment of death, if we are united to Him through the development of the filial grace which has been given us and binds us closely to Him, we shall enter into the rhythm of the Blessed Trinity and share in its works, privileges and happiness.

This is our end, this is the happiness of heaven; not only to see God from a distance but to be God by participation, to perform the works of knowledge and love which are the works of the Word, and in this way to share the happiness and life of the Word. In other words, our destiny is to enter with Him as *actors*, not merely spectators, into the rhythm of the Trinitarian life and to share the happiness of God Himself, in sharing that of the Word incarnate.

Essential exercise of the Christian vocation

For us, this is what prayer is: our essential duty. We can see now why it should be an obligation for us, and why Christ taught us this by His example. He gave the greater part of His time in this world to prayer, the exercise of union. Did He need it for Himself? No, since He possessed the hypostatic union. But He wanted to instruct us by His deeds and example, by His attitude and activity, as well as by His words.

In this world Christ Jesus gave Himself primarily to the exercise of union. Our life in this world, our Christian life, even our earthly life — let us not distinguish between the Christian life and human or earthly life — should also be an exercise of union like that of Christ, and consequently our prayer should be a prayer of union, a contemplative prayer. This is the truth: our duty lies here.

It is sometimes surprising to see, in works which are otherwise truly inspired and which bring us precious truths, that prayer is presented as accessory, so to speak, something for feastdays or reserved to certain souls who have the time for it, or as they say, the vocation. Prayer is the essential exercise of every Christian's vocation. It has sometimes been said that contemplative prayer is egotistical, turning the soul in upon itself. This is to forget the catechism definition. The prayer that focuses the soul upon itself, in order to analyze its impressions, is not a prayer. Prayer is an exercise of union, a lifting of the soul to God, union with God; to think it merely accessory is to be ignorant of the essence of the Christian life.

From this point of view, then, the prayer of union remains for us a basic, fundamental obligation. And if certain souls are especially dedicated to contemplative prayer because of their vocation, if our Lord gives them a vocation to that, if He has even willed that certain Institutes or religious Orders should be especially dedicated to this kind of prayer, it is because He has willed that His teaching should always remain alive and actual before the eyes of the Christian faithful. But this does not exempt any

Christian from the essential obligation of prayer, contemplative prayer, the prayer of union.

III — THE PRAYER OF JESUS, HEAD OF THE MYSTICAL BODY

Christ Jesus is not only the Man-God. He is also the Head of the Mystical Body. Jesus has redeemed us by His suffering, given us divine life through His sacraments; and in thus sharing His divine life, He has redeemed us.

His life in us

The grace which we receive in baptism is the life of Christ, which is given to us through our participation in the mystery of His suffering and death. When we receive Communion the divine life of the risen Christ penetrates us. He causes it to penetrate us through the Eucharist in which He is at once living and immolated. This divine life which Christ pours into us unites us with Him: it is the life of Christ. You remember what St. Augustine said of Christ giving Himself in the Eucharist: we consume Him, but in reality it is He who absorbs us.[19] He puts His life in us and we become *Him*. Through this life which He gives us, a union is realized between Him and ourselves.

In this way Christ constitutes a new reality. His overflowing life, which gives and diffuses itself, and the new reality constituted by this diffusion of divine life in our souls, is the Church, the whole Christ.[20] He gives us His life, we receive the Holy Spirit, we become other Christs, we become Christ. We enter into Him, He enters into us, we are possessed by Him. That is the Church.

By this diffusion of divine life, particularly through the Holy Eucharist, we enter into Christ, we become Him. But at the same time Christ possesses us. In the Church there is not only the union of ourselves with Christ, but also the union of Christ with us: the union is mutual. We receive His life and He assumes what we are. Christ has taken on humanity, and in taking on humanity He has taken on all humanities. He especially takes on the humanity of those who are united with Him through grace. He gives us His life and He takes our human nature. Consequently there is an intercommunication between Christ and us.

Our sin is laid upon Him

This mutual communication which enriches us with Christ and His life, which identifies us with Him and makes the presence of the Holy Spirit in our souls more vital — as it is vital in Him — all this means that Christ takes on our misery, our human nature with all that it is. He has taken on everything but sin,[21] but He has taken on sin's consequences. This is precisely how the Redemption took effect.

How are we ourselves purified? We are purified because Christ *assumes* the consequences of sin which are in us. This is affirmed by Isaiah.[22] He has taken on our infirmities, our miseries. When St. John the Baptist sees Christ Jesus, he names Him, saying, "Behold the Lamb of God, who *takes away* the sin of the world."[23] Jesus wipes out sin by taking it upon Himself.

We could say, to use a comparison which seems a bit common but is to my mind very expressive, that Christ, in making contact with us, becomes like a sheet of blotting paper. We are stained, we bear the consequences of sin. Christ is an immaculate sheet which places itself upon our humanity and thus takes away our misery. He has taken on our infirmities.

The struggle in Jesus

This infirmity of ours which Christ has taken upon Himself causes Him suffering, and this gives us the opportunity to study another form and consequence of the prayer of Christ.

Christ, coming into this world, takes upon His

own humanity the sin of our humanity — His divinity cannot be weighed down by it — and suffers the consequences of this sin. This is why the drama of the Passion begins from the very first moment of Christ's existence. As He assumes the sin of humanity — not this or that sin, but *peccatum mundi*, the sin of the world — immediately there is set up in Him, by the fact of His hypostatic union, a painful opposition between the sin, which is not His but ours, and the divinity, the holiness which is His. Immediately He becomes a victim.

This is the suffering of Christ, the suffering of the Passion, to which the Letter to the Hebrews alludes when it says that He learned the value of obedience through suffering.[24] God willed Christ to be our redeemer and He obeyed: He accomplished this by taking upon Himself our sin. And this suffering was a form of experiential knowledge.

Two contrary movements are set up — yet not contraries, since the divinity penetrates Him continually: on the one hand His humanity receives floods of the divinity which penetrate Him, and on the other hand there is this movement of sin which mounts in Him, this stain He has taken on with His extreme sensibility. There is no cloth so efficient in touching and removing a stain as the sensibility of Christ in coming into contact with our sin. There is therefore this opposition, these contraries, this struggle within Him.

Agonized prayer in Gethsemane

The peak, we might say the crucial point in this struggle, will be Gethsemane. Until now, Jesus has endured both elements, but in a kind of balance. As they cross the brook Cedron and enter Gethsemane, Jesus says, "This is the hour of the power of darkness."[25] He allows free scope now to all the power of evil, to sin itself as stain, hatred, opposition to God. Does He not still enjoy the hypostatic union and the vision? Yes, but He allows sin its full force, allows all its power to invade Him, to flood His senses, His body, His sensibility, His imagination, His intellect, in brief, His whole human nature.

We may say that at this moment Christ Jesus enjoys the happiness of the intuitive vision of God and at the same time suffers the pain of hell. It is hell assaulting heaven, and in this combat the field of battle is the humanity of Christ. Clearly there must be an explosion. It is the humanity of Christ that bursts open, hence the sweat of blood.[26] Jesus falls with His face to the ground and utters loud cries. This is the prayer of Christ.

The agonized prayer of Gethsemane reduces Christ to loud cries. He who could bear the weight of divinity feels His weakness and falls with His face to the earth. He goes to seek help from His Apostles: "Could you not watch one hour with Me?"[27] He staggers as it were between the grotto where He is praying and the place where He left them, seeking help; and God sends an angel to strengthen Him.[28]

Prayer continued in the Church

It is this prayer of suffering, this grief-filled prayer whose agony is caused by contradiction, of hell's assault on the heaven within Him, it is this prayer that is redemptive. Christ, now in heaven, dies no more, the apostle St. Paul tells us,[29] but He has left to His Church the anguish resulting from the opposition between sin and divinity. He has left to Christians the responsibility of realizing the prayer of union; He has left to us also the role of continuing the agonized prayer of Gethsemane.

Here we are not speaking of any torment which we might endure solely for our own purification. This is a suffering which continues the Redemption, a suffering by which the Church and souls fill up what is lacking to the Passion of Christ.[30] The merit of Christ's Passion is infinite; what is lacking is its application to souls.

The Church is in Christ. She must live the whole Christ, realize the whole Christ, His state of union, His state of prayer. She must also realize His activity and His principal function, His redemptive role. She does this painfully, through prayer. If the Church is destined to continue Christ's life through

His activity, she must also continue His agonizing prayer in a still greater measure. The proportion is indicated to us by the time Jesus devoted to prayer and by the efficacy of this role of His.

Here we touch on the drama of contemplative prayer and the need for monasteries and for contemplative prayer. What did the great contemplatives such as St. Teresa of Avila and St. Thérèse of the Child Jesus do? They continued the prayer of Gethsemane. St. Teresa of Avila says that for long years, every evening before going to sleep she contemplated Jesus in Gethsemane and prolonged His prayer.[31]

St. Thérèse of the Child Jesus did the same thing. She endured, especially at the end of her life, the struggle between the modern sin of unbelief and pride and the holiness and grace she bore within her.[32] Obviously she did not do this as Christ Himself had, for she did not possess the hypostatic union. However lofty her sanctity, she did not bear the sin of the world. But she bore the sin of our times. And because of this, because she too was a "cloth" wiping this sin from souls, she was redemptive, a co-redeemer.

In our day we admire the fact that she is a great wonder-worker, that she can enlighten and save so many souls, and that she is the great missionary and apostle of modern times. Yet all this is so, not because she engaged in activities but because she engaged in Christ's essential function, the redemptive role of taking away the sin of the world.

GREAT CHRISTIAN TRUTHS

This brings us to the close of these discussions. It is not for me to explain the mystery of Christ exhaustively. I have spoken to you of luminous clouds, luminous rays which pierce the night at least momentarily and allow us to advance further into the prayer of Christ and to see what we need to see of its nature and usefulness. From this, I propose to draw some practical conclusions.

Fundamental activity

The first is, that we ought to pray much. We must not be Christians who think that reciting our morning and night prayers and assisting absent-mindedly, or even fervently, at Sunday Mass, is all and more than we are obliged to do, since some of our neighbors do even less.

Our true life, which will never end, will be a life of union with God, and we are here on this earth to prepare for it. If we reach heaven and do not know how to pray, we will probably have to learn, and we may not make the grade because we will not know where to begin. Prayer is an art we cannot acquire in heaven! God will say, "For fifty, sixty years, maybe more, you have had the means at your disposal for praying and uniting yourself to Me, and you haven't done it? You have buried this precious talent? You have not traded with it?"[33]

The Christian life is not only a moral life, it does not consist merely in avoiding this or that sin. It consists primarily in doing something positive. We do not develop our physical life by avoiding microbes; we develop it by the exercise of our vital functions and by nourishing our vital energies with proper food. Our vital Christian energies are grace, and sonship of God, and the consequent carrying out in this world of our role as His children. Our performance will be imperfect, but we carry on in faith and in reality. Our role as God's children consists in uniting ourselves to Him, and, with God the Father, breathing Love, as St. John of the Cross says,[34] breathing the Holy Spirit.

Allow me to insist on this point. In our day even good Christians are sometimes oriented to roles which are important but secondary. It is sometimes suggested that the exercise of charity means primarily the exercise of social charity. This is not true. Social charity is included among our duties, but it is a false interpretation of the Gospel to think that being a Christian means primarily exercising social charity.

Charity is what unites us to God. Our Lord asks us to exercise charity toward our neighbors by supernaturalizing what we do, by seeing in them images of God, or performing acts of charity with the object of drawing them to the essential functions of children of God and thereby leading them to the Blessed Trinity. Our charity should have an apostolic aim: to lead others along the way, not just to Sunday Mass, but to the Blessed Trinity.

This is not reserved to a few specialists who have the time, or to a few monks or religious who have the taste for it. It is a Christian truth. It is our family life, our intimate life. Quite simply, it is our Christian life. We need therefore to give our children the means, the instruction, which will orient them to this Trinitarian life in which we should all share and which is our goal. We should exercise ourselves in union and orient our personal, family, and social life to this goal of participation in Trinitarian life.

Prayer which saves

If we wish to save the world, we must do it, certainly, by our actions and our apostolate, as Christ did: He devoted three years to that. But in the end He saved the world through His sufferings and agonizing prayer. The great means of saving the world is to take on its sin in an efficacious way. Our compassion should not be merely humanitarian, but Christian. We ought to impregnate ourselves with God, tending toward the hypostatic union not in order to bring it about in ourselves, but in order to bring about union with Christ. This union enables us to take on the sins of others in a way that is effective and fruitful. We become capable of taking on ourselves the sin of the humanity which surrounds us, these brothers and sisters of ours who are so close to us.

We do indeed have the duty of relieving misery, feeding the hungry, giving drink to the thirsty, and sheltering the homeless. But I believe that our greatest concern should be to give souls the true nourishment which is Christ, God, and the true drink flowing from the rock which is Christ.[35] We ought to provide for souls, not so much a shelter for the few days or years they will spend in this world, but rather the shelter and refuge of the Blessed Trinity, where they will spend all eternity.

This is what Christian truth makes plain to us. This truth is not meant to be preached to individuals here and there or to some specially favored group of people. It is, in a word, Christian truth.

Let us remember this. I ask it of the Blessed Virgin, who lived this truth profoundly. Pondering on the teaching of our Lord, she buried herself in solitude when there was a whole world to be converted. She set out on her mission as mediatrix, she set out into solitude to continue the true and profound life of Christ, the life of prayer in silence.

I also ask St. Thérèse of the Child Jesus, St. Teresa of Avila, and St. John of the Cross, who pointed out this way and recalled for us these great Christian truths, to root them deeply in our souls through this word which is spoken to us in the name of the Church in the difficult times through which we are passing.

We feel the world invaded by the powers of evil. Sin is very near, rising on the horizon with admirably organized human power. At physical, psychological and intellectual levels, the devil himself utilizes a power higher than ours, and normally it assures him at least apparent victories. How can we overcome him? We can only do it by supernatural means. Before His death, Jesus said to us: "I send you out as sheep in the midst of wolves, and they will put you to death...."[36] He gave His disciples a program. He made predictions which at first sight seemed hardly encouraging, but He also said to them, "Be of good cheer, I have overcome the world."[37] How did He overcome it? By taking its sin upon Himself, by prayer.

In these times, in face of the dangers threatening us, what is our reason for hope? It is of course Christ, the prayer of Christ who ever lives in heaven to intercede for us.[38] Our prayer rests upon the prayer of Christ. He is ever living in His Church.

As for the Holy Spirit dwelling in our souls, what does He do? The apostle St. Paul, with his keen ear, has heard Him, apprehended Him, ever praying, uttering unspeakable groans.[39] What is left for us to do ourselves, to assure not only the salvation of our own souls but the salvation of Christians, of the world? We are to unite our personal prayer and our activity with the prayer of the Holy Spirit in our souls and with the ever efficacious prayer of Christ in heaven. This is how we shall carry off the victory, for ourselves, our brethren, for the whole world.

Notes

[1] Cf. Lk 11:1-4.

[2] Cf. St. Teresa of Avila, *The Way of Perfection*, chs. 21-44.

[3] Jesus Christ is true God and true man. The Son of God, the second Person of the Blessed Trinity, united Himself to our human nature while retaining His divine nature. To explain this mystery, theology uses the expression "hypostatic union," or union according to the Person (in Greek, *hypostasis*). Realized at the moment of the Incarnation, this union is henceforth indissoluble, that is, permanent and definitive.

[4] From the Greek, *theos*, God, and *andros*, man.

[5] Cf. Ex 13:21-22.

[6] Cf. "The Mystery of God," 28, n. 16.

[7] Cf. St. John of the Cross, *The Spiritual Canticle*, str. 37, 549-553.

[8] Cf. Lk 2:52.

[9] Cf. Heb 5:8.

[10] Cf. Mt 4:1ff.

[11] Cf. Lk 5:16.

[12] Cf. Lk 6:12.
[13] Cf. Lk 21:37.
[14] Cf. Rm 8:34 and Heb 7:25-26.
[15] Cf. Lk 3:21-22.
[16] Cf. Jn 1:33.
[17] Cf. Lk 9:28ff.
[18] The expression is found in Mt 17:5.
[19] Cf. St. Augustine, *Confessions*, VII, 10.
[20] Bossuet, 4th Letter, "To a Young Lady of Metz," 28.
[21] Cf. Heb 4:15.
[22] Cf. Is 53:4-5.
[23] Cf. Jn 1:29.
[24] Cf. Heb 5:8.
[25] Cf. Lk 22:53.
[26] Cf. Lk 22:44.
[27] Cf. Mt 26:40.
[28] Cf. Lk 22:43.
[29] Cf. Rm 6:9.
[30] Cf. Col 1:24.
[31] Cf. St. Teresa of Avila, *Life*, ch. 9.
[32] Cf. *Manuscript C*, 5 r° ff.
[33] Cf. Mt 25:14ff.
[34] *The Spiritual Canticle*, str. 39, 557-558.
[35] Cf. 1 Cor 10:4.
[36] Cf. Mt 10:16ff.
[37] Jn 16:33.
[38] Rm 8:34.
[39] Cf. Rm 8:26.

Part Three — In the Grip of the Spirit

Building the Kingdom

The action of the Spirit in our times

The Holy Spirit dwelling within the Church never manifests His presence and power more palpably than when encountering the pressure of adverse forces, and when it seems as though these would annihilate Him or drive Him forth. To St. Paul, who complained of the buffeting of Satan, the Lord replied, "My grace is sufficient for you, for my power is made perfect in weakness."[1] Enlightened by this word and by his experience, the great apostle said, "For the sake of Christ I am content with weaknesses, insults, hardships, persecutions and calamities; for when I am weak, then I am strong."[2]

A glance at the history of the Church, especially the history of the persecutions during the first centuries, or again the religious history of the sixteenth and seventeenth centuries, suffices to show the application of this law of the Holy Spirit's action in the Church.

It is too soon to form a definitive judgment

about our own era. Undoubtedly we are living through painful times. There is the sorrow of the dechristianization of the masses, which seems to be on the increase, and the many violent struggles in which the world is engaged. Finally, there is the anguish caused by the threat of Russian and Asiatic communism. This last, encouraged by its successes, has already armed hundreds of millions of the men under its domination with its mystique of the destruction of all Christian civilization. But the fear aroused by this threat, and the psychosis which it can lead to, should not blind us and prevent us from recognizing and appreciating at its true worth the action of the Holy Spirit in our times. He creates and sustains in souls a need for the absolute and a desire for a deep spiritual life and for the apostolate.

We see numerous recruits joining the new Institutes which the Holy Spirit is bringing to birth in the Church. They join because these Institutes offer them a means of entering upon the sublime adventure of a life totally and exclusively consecrated to the service of God and neighbor. A new springtime is astir within the Church today, in the life-giving breath of the Holy Spirit. He is causing the sap to rise and new shoots to push up. His breath is swelling the promising buds and causing them to burst into flower. But it can also precipitate death and scandal. The aged Simeon, who held Christ Jesus in his arms on the day of His presentation in the Temple, declared that He would be the light of the nations and the glory of His people, but also that He would lead to the fall and the rise of many.[3]

As happens with natural gifts, so is it with the highest gifts of God. They are given to us for our salvation, but if misused they can lead to our loss. It would be difficult and delicate to insist on the point and to make applications here. However, we should recognize, and we ought to admit, that there have been sincere and generous souls, apparently moved by the breath of the Spirit blowing through the Church of our times, who have gone astray. We keep them in our affection and our prayer, but we need to avoid their mistakes and falls.

It pertains to the hierarchy to guide us in the difficult and at times perilous area of response to the breath of the Holy Spirit, that is, in determining what is God's mind and will for our times and for each one of us. The Sovereign Pontiff does this by means of his enlightening encyclicals which discuss the many problems which preoccupy us. The bishops give out practical directives for apostolic action. The first duty of the Christian is to submit to this teaching of the Church and to obey the directives she gives.

This duty of submission, a primordial one, does not dispense us from studying, with the objective of clarifying the Church's directives. We are encouraged also to explore the mind of God expressed in Holy Scripture and Christian tradition, especially apostolic tradition. The Holy Spirit dwelling within the Church is to be found in each of its parts, hence in every soul. We can count on His help for this work of research and study, as we pursue it with respect for the authority which He has established and in submission to the authority He has given to the Church.

In this conference my only intention is to throw light on a problem of the apostolate which is one of the most delicate problems of our time, the problem of respect and perfect submission to the Church. I do not wish to discuss the value of various methods in a polemical way, nor to treat the problem in all its dimensions, but simply to recall some fundamental truths which appear to me to be enlightening, and are sometimes forgotten.

I — THE AIM OF THE APOSTOLATE

It is said of Marshal Foch that when faced with a military problem to be resolved, he asked himself and his chief-of-staff this question: "What is at stake?" In other words, "What is the situation and what is the goal you are proposing?" It seems a rather banal question, but if it is overlooked we risk great confusion.

Let us therefore ask this question in regard to

the apostolate: What is at stake? Let us fine tune the question: What is the purpose of the apostolate? Under what general and practical conditions should it be carried on? This is the problem we are considering today. In our second conference, we shall see what the apostolate consists in, and find its definition. Later we shall study the means proper to the apostolate. All this, in the light of the Gospel and the teaching and example of the Apostles.

Jesus came to inaugurate the Kingdom

What is the goal of the apostolate? The apostolate's purpose is to continue within the Church the work of Christ Jesus and His Apostles. What did Christ do? He came into this world to establish the Kingdom of God.

The purpose of the apostolate, therefore, is to establish the Kingdom of God. A glance at the Gospel suffices to convince us of this. St. John the Baptist is sent to prepare for the preaching of Christ and he does it by announcing that the Kingdom of God is at hand.[4] He invites the crowds to prepare for this Kingdom by penance and good works, for only by these means can they hope to enter it.

The greater part of Jesus' preaching will be on this theme: the Kingdom of God. Jesus will indicate its laws and requirements, especially in His parables.

There is no doubt in anyone's mind that Jesus has come to establish the Kingdom of God. The Apostles expect to be its first officials[5] and will be vying with each other up to the last moment of Christ's earthly life to ascertain which one of those chosen by God to be Apostles will be the leader of the band.[6]

In the presence of Roman power which has established its rule in Judea, and before Pontius Pilate, Jesus proclaims Himself a King.[7] This is the reason for His condemnation. On His cross will be written, *Jesus Nazarenus Rex Judaeorum*, "Jesus of Nazareth, King of the Jews."[8]

The Kingdom is Christ's life in us

Let us continue our inquiry, asking: What is this Kingdom of God which Christ came to establish?

Recall the declaration of Jesus before Pilate, namely that His Kingdom is not of this world. After having affirmed that He is a King, Jesus adds: "If my Kingdom were of this world, my servants would fight that I might not be handed over to the Jews; but my Kingdom is not from the world."[9] This is a very clear declaration which ought to be enough to prevent us from dreaming of the earthly domination of Christ or of the Sacred Heart over the entire world.

The Apostles, who had cultivated up to the

end this myth of an earthly kingdom, hoping to become its chief ministers under the universal rule of Christ, received no answer to that final question which they put to Jesus a few moments before His Ascension.[10] And yet the archangel Gabriel had indeed announced to the Virgin Mary that the Son to be born of her would sit upon the throne of David His father, and that His Kingdom would have no end.[11]

In order to explain this apparent contradiction between the language of the promise and its realization, we need to remember that human language is not perfectly adapted to the supernatural. The Holy Spirit and theology can only describe supernatural and spiritual realities through the use of symbols and analogies. Do we not do the same thing ourselves when we want to explain to children, or even to an adult audience, things they do not know or have never seen, and which we cannot show them? We give examples, symbols, familiar ideas, and we try with the help of what is known to move to the reality we are explaining.

"The Kingdom of God is like a grain of mustard seed," Jesus will say,[12] without however wishing to imply a perfect resemblance between the Kingdom of God and the mustard seed. The analogy between the two terms bears on only one very specific characteristic of each, a characteristic which the parable brings out clearly. We shall even have to say that the

Kingdom of God which Jesus came to establish is not like the kingdoms we are familiar with, although it is truly a kingdom.

What is it, then? Let us ask the apostle St. Paul, the great theologian of Christ, the apostle who proclaims himself the herald of the great mystery hidden in past ages and now to be revealed and fulfilled.[13] This mystery of the Kingdom of God is not manifested to others except in parables. It is for him to give us the understanding of it which he himself has received. And thus he discloses the fact that God, who willed to create all things through His Word, decreed after the fall of man in the earthly Paradise to restore all things through His incarnate Word, Christ Jesus.[14]

"For in Him all the fulness of God was pleased to dwell, and through Him to reconcile to Himself all things, whether on earth or in heaven, making peace by the blood of His cross."[15] God placed the Word incarnate, Jesus, at the summit of all things, says the apostle, "and He has put all things under His feet and has made Him the head over all things for the Church, which is His body, the fulness of Him who fills all in all."[16] In these few words, obscure because so packed with truth, St. Paul places before us the entire plan of the mysteries of the Incarnation, the Redemption, and the Church.

The Word becomes flesh, and is Christ Jesus. He comes to save us, to ransom us, and He does it through the sacrifice of Calvary. The blood which He sheds is the blood of the new Covenant of God with men. This blood is our cleansing and our life. As the Word, Christ Jesus gives us His light, as Savior He purifies us, and as Word incarnate He gives us His life and His grace.

We receive this life and grace through the sacraments, and more especially through the principal one, Holy Communion. This life of Christ descends into our souls, it is given to us in baptism, and it develops progressively. Because it is charity it unites us to Christ, identifies us with Him, and establishes between ourselves and Him very close bonds. At every instant Christ pours life into our souls, and unites us to Himself in such a way that we form, together with Him, a new reality, which is the Mystical Body, the whole Christ, the Church.

The Christ who unites us to Himself, of whom we are the completion and prolongation, reigns over our souls because we are united to Him. He is truly our King. We are under His rule, under His action; we become His subjects, we become "Him." He is our King, our Master, our "all," to use the expressive language of the apostle St. Paul.[17]

The Kingdom of God is the whole Christ, the Church. This Kingdom is therefore primarily spiritual, since it is constituted by Christ and by the life of grace which He pours into our souls. It is spiritual because the Holy Spirit animates it. He is its soul.

Its growth follows the concrete conditions of existence

But this Mystical Body of Christ, in order to adapt itself perfectly to our human condition and to fulfill its mission in us and in the world, is also built up externally into a perfectly organized, visible society. This visible society, the Church, by reason of its mission which is to lead souls to their last end, to lead them to God, to draw them to Christ and maintain them in union with Him, has a function to exercise in the world. It has rights which it is able to exercise in relation to other societies, by reason of its universality and the excellence of its mission. The Kingdom of God is therefore the Mystical Body of Christ, and a visible society.

This Mystical Body of Christ is always in the process of being built up. It is unceasingly being built and will go on being built until the end of time, as long as humanity perdures, since it is made for humanity and must lead us all to Christ and to salvation through Him. The apostolate, begun by the Apostles, must continue until the end of time. This apostolate has for its end the building up of the Mystical Body of Christ until the end of time, and, as the apostle St. Paul says, until we all attain to the unity of the faith and of the knowledge of the Son of God, to mature manhood, to the measure of the stature of the fulness of Christ, which God has willed from all eternity.[18] This, briefly, is what the Kingdom of God is.

II — THE CONDITIONS OF THE SPIRITUAL COMBAT

This Kingdom of God develops under certain conditions. One of the most important of them, announced by Jesus, is that it will be hindered in its expansion, its construction, and its upbuilding by the enemy, the one who sows cockle after the sower has sown good grain, while men sleep.[19] It will be hindered by the power of evil, by Satan, who also has his kingdom. Concerning the kingdom of Satan we have to say the same thing we said just now about the Kingdom of Christ, namely that the word "kingdom" should not be used in a strict sense. It simply indicates the exercise of a certain power.

A formidable power

What is this kingdom of Satan? We know from the Gospel that the devil exists. Currently, some claim that they do not believe in the devil, while others see him everywhere. What is the devil? A fallen angel who has become a power for evil. Since he is a fallen angel he remains a spirit and consequently retains the power of a spirit, exercising a certain control over matter. He has been gifted with a penetrating intellect and is also able to acquire a certain experiential knowledge.

The power of the devil is to be feared therefore, and all the more since the demons are numerous. Among them there is a kind of alliance in opposing the building up of the Mystical Body of Christ. God has willed and does will that the devil exercise his powerful opposition.

Let us recall, in the Gospel, the parable of the cockle and the good wheat. The wheat was planted by the sower. Then the enemy came in the night to sow cockle. When both came up, the servants went to find their master and told him that cockle had been sown in his field. They proposed to uproot it. The master refused. He told them to let both wheat and cockle grow together, so that the wheat could come up in the midst of contradiction. When harvest time came, the servants would separate the wheat from the cockle. In the meantime, both must grow up together. This is the teaching of Jesus. Let us not ask God, therefore, to get rid of the devil. He has his providential role.

St. John of the Cross goes even further. Commenting on the Book of Job, he tells us that God gives the devil certain knowledge, certain means of tempting the just. The saint explains this remark by saying that when a soul receives supernatural favors,

God makes them known to the devil so that he may imitate and counterfeit them.[20] This is precise and valuable information. The devil has a providential role.

The combat of Jesus

In order to be aware of the devil's opposition to the Church and his activity in obstructing the growth of the Mystical Body of Christ, we need not turn to spectacular or extraordinary stories. Let us simply go to the Gospel. There we find a description of the devil's activity.

What do we see in the life of our Lord? As long as Jesus is in Nazareth, the devil does not appear. Is he there? Yes, probably. Does he know that Jesus is the Son of God? The Fathers and Doctors of the Church differ on this point. It is a controversial question.

But now Jesus leaves Nazareth and goes into the desert to prepare for His public life by prayer and fasting. He is driven there by the Spirit, the Gospel tells us.[21] What does He find in the desert? In the desert, there is God. People go to the desert in search of God. But the devil also is there. He prowls around Jesus, puzzled about the identity of this person who has left Nazareth and His family and who, in this solitude, has fasted for forty days and is plunged in profound prayer. The devil then receives power to tempt Him.

The temptation is described in detail for us in the Gospel, certainly for our instruction. As the evangelists, and especially Matthew, describe it, we can observe a progression, which reveals the devil's cleverness.[22]

He confronts Jesus, this marvelous, extraordinary person whose power he suspects, but whose identity he is not yet sure of. He begins by tempting Him at the sense level. Jesus has not eaten for forty days, and the devil suggests, "If you are the Son of God, command that these stones be turned into bread." He is tempting Him to both gluttony and pride.

He is repulsed by Jesus, who answers, "'It is written, "Man shall not live by bread alone, but by every word that proceeds from the mouth of God."' Then the devil took Him to the holy city, and set Him on the pinnacle of the temple, and said to Him, 'If you are the Son of God, throw yourself down, for it is written, "He will give His angels charge of you… and on their hands they will bear you up, lest you strike your foot against a stone."'"

This is a far more subtle temptation. The devil seems certain now that he is dealing with the almighty Son of God, and he is going to try to get Him to use His omnipotence. So he tells Him to cast Himself down: If you are the Son of God, you can count on the assistance of the angels. Jesus repulses the temptation: "Jesus said to him, 'Again it is written, "You shall not tempt the Lord your God."'" Here a revelation is being made to the devil. He knows now that he is dealing with the Messiah.

Now, with this knowledge, "the devil took Him to a very high mountain, and showed Him all the kingdoms of the world and the glory of them; and he said to Him, 'All these I will give you, if you will fall down and worship me.'" The devil knows Scripture. He is aware that universal dominion is promised to the Messiah. Therefore he proposes to ally himself with Jesus, to give Him external power over the entire world. The Gospel tells us that Jesus repulses this third temptation. "Then Jesus said to him, 'Begone, Satan! for it is written, "You shall worship the Lord your God and Him only shall you serve."'" This is the description of the struggle in which the devil engages Jesus.

Jesus then begins His teaching, and the devil withdraws. What will he do? He will be near Jesus. Particularly while He is preaching in Galilee, we shall see demons surrounding Him. Jesus drives the demons out of bodies, out of souls. They proclaim Him to be the Son of God and He silences them.

It seems as if Jesus has definitively overcome the devil, that there is nothing more he can do. Jesus Himself will tell us in the Gospel[23] that when the devil is overcome he takes refuge in the desert, in waterless wastes, and there gathers other demons to continue the combat. The devil's tactics are revealed here. He goes to seek other demons, and takes up the battle with new tactics.

How will he fight? He knows well that he can do nothing against Christ directly. But while Jesus continues His preaching, in Galilee and Jerusalem, and works miracles, the devil is playing his own hidden game. He is a very clever manipulator, who can act upon matter and upon man as long as he is in the body. He is a keen psychologist. He knows human proclivities, desires, weaknesses and energies, and can exploit them in a remarkable way. While Jesus is preaching, the devil works among various sects, such as the Pharisees and Sadducees, and among various political powers.

He is also extraordinarily clever in manipulating crowds, and is a master of mob psychology. While Jesus is giving His message, the devil's activity is on the increase. We sense this strongly, especially in the Gospel of St. John. The opposition grows under cover, in the dark. Already there are doubts, discussions, and parties are forming. The devil even gains a foothold in the apostolic college, where he will find a traitor, Judas, to deliver up the Master.[24]

At the end of three years, during which Jesus completes and clarifies His mission and develops His message, proclaiming it openly and proving by His deeds and miracles that He is the Son of God, the devil on his side has been working in the dark. "This is your hour, and the power of darkness," says Jesus.[25] It seems as if Jesus will triumph, and in fact He does triumph on Palm Sunday in Jerusalem. And yet the hour of the power of darkness has struck. In Gethsemane the devil will go so far as to attack Christ's humanity. Here we have a personal attack by the power of darkness upon the humanity of Christ.

What happens in Gethsemane is a mystery which we shall never be able to fathom. There are such human and psychological contrasts, such spiritual contrasts, that we can only study it from afar, while adoring Christ in His abasement and at the same time in the might of His victory. Tremendous force is exerted upon Christ here, and this force, this pressure of the devil upon His humanity, causes the bloody sweat of Gethsemane.[26]

And this is only the beginning, we might say, of the drama. The following day, Good Friday, will show how the devil has succeeded externally, in winning over the crowds and the Council of the Elders, scribes and Pharisees who will league together to demand the death of Christ. And we know the outcome. It is Calvary, where truly the devil's power triumphs.

On various occasions Jesus has called the devil "the prince of this world."[27] He has also foretold his defeat. And now the devil triumphs on Calvary. His action destroys everything. The Apostles have fled, Judas has betrayed Jesus, and there is no one, not one voice raised in His defense. It seems as if Jesus' work has been completely demolished.

The Church in the footsteps of Jesus

In the life of Christ and on Calvary the activity of the devil within the Church is already foreshadowed. Just now, in speaking of the Kingdom of God, I said that the Church is the Mystical Body of Christ. It is the whole Christ, Christ Himself, the prolongation of Christ in time, Christ who grows unceasingly until the end of time. This growth, this development, this building up of Christ will take place according to the same laws which governed His life on earth. Outward circumstances may change, but the laws will remain the same. The life of Christ will develop in the same way, with the same contradictions. This is what I should like to emphasize in the present conference.

I should like first of all to note a fundamental truth, namely, that the Church is the whole Christ, and is developing unceasingly. I should also like to stress the intelligent, constant action of the devil against the Church through the ages. Some people say they do not believe in the devil, or they seek extraordinary manifestations of him. These may exist, they do in every age, but the activity of the devil is not found primarily in individual cases of possession which we can observe here or there. His is an intelligent activity, working upon individuals and upon crowds.

This highly intelligent activity makes use of all the energies and forces of nature, and of all inventions. It operates at the psychological, psychic, and intellectual levels. The devil's activity makes him the prince of this world today, as he was in the time of Christ. He has no less hatred for the Church, the prolongation of Christ, the whole Christ, than he had for Christ.

What are the phases of this struggle? This combat, which goes on now and will go on until the end of time, witnesses the development of Christ. Christ triumphs, for He develops. Each day the life of Christ flows through the sacraments, through Communion; it flows into the intimate depths of souls with Christ. Each day the Church is nourished with Christ.

The Holy Spirit lives within the Church and does His work there. He who is its Builder develops it, and consequently the Church grows without ceasing. It triumphs in this daily growth, and many souls by their death join the Church Triumphant, where there is no fear of further combat.

But in this world the Holy Spirit continues His work, and the Church spreads. At the same time

Satan's power rages, an intelligent power which attempts to block and prevent the expansion and upbuilding of the Church. The devil is the prince of this world. As in the time of Christ, he obtains victories, apparent victories but real nonetheless. In the measure in which we advance toward the endtime, even as Christ develops and becomes more powerful in His Church, so too the devil acquires experience and consequently develops and improves his weapons, which become more and more inimical to the Church. And he obtains his apparent victories.

This is the truth. This world belongs to the devil. It is here in this world that he gains his apparent victories. May we think that the day will come when Christ will triumph in this world, and the devil will win no more victories? This is a mystery, but we can once more obtain light on it from the Gospel.

What do we read there? This is what Jesus Himself says: "When the Son of Man comes, will He find faith on earth?"[28] Again He says, in St. Matthew, "And because wickedness is multiplied, most men's love will grow cold. But he who endures to the end will be saved."[29] And speaking of the endtime, Jesus says, "For the sake of the elect, those days will be shortened."[30]

If we study the life of Christ and seek to understand the life of the Church by analogy, we will ask: What will its end be like? It seems to me that its end could well be a Calvary. Why dream of victory when Christ had no triumph but that of the Cross? The prolongation of Christ, the Church at the end of time, could be, and it seems to me will be, like Christ in His life here on earth. Such is the Gospel truth.

We ought to look this truth in the face. It is not clearly revealed in the precise terms I have used, but we can nevertheless deduce it from what is told to us. Why should we forever delude ourselves with dreams of earthly triumphs? Why forever encourage each other, saying, "Tomorrow things will be better, tomorrow we shall win"? We would be doing what the Apostles did, cultivating a myth. "But if we don't say this, we will lose courage...." But I do not see why, for the sake of encouragement, we should tell ourselves lies.

It suffices to look the truth in the face, and the truth is beautiful. Christ is developing. Each day He triumphs, but He triumphs in suffering and in sorrow. He triumphs in blood and defeat.

Salvation in hope: the victory of Christ

His great victory: what will it be? Let us listen again to Jesus, let us not follow our imaginations and yield to the persistent desire to triumph and dominate. Humiliated before the high priest and before men who would not recognize Him when their mission was precisely to prepare for His coming and to recognize Him, Christ says: "Hereafter you will see the Son of Man seated at the right hand of Power, and coming on the clouds of heaven, to judge the living and the dead."[31]

This is the triumph we may and should look forward to. I know very well that people will say to us at times, "Oh yes, you people think of nothing but the next world!" But if it is the truth, let us think of it. We may think of the Church's triumph occurring in a sense each day, but let us think also of this great triumph in the end.

The early Christians in the Church of the first centuries often thought about the Parousia, the final triumph. They believed that Christ would return soon. And the apostle St. Paul sustained them in this hope.[32] As for us, let us look to this end, this salvation in hope. Let us look to our own salvation. We do not have to await the Last Judgment in order to triumph ourselves. We triumph on the day of our death when we enter into the life of Christ, the life of God, the face to face vision.

But the triumph of the Church will come on the last day. In my opinion the Last Judgment will not be, as it is so often unfortunately depicted, a rendering of accounts, an examination by some sort of inspector who will come to look over all our little affairs and weigh them as the world looks on. No, the Last Judgment is the triumph of Christ, who descends in all His glory and who enfolds and penetrates all who have believed in Him with His glory. This is the truth we ought to think about....

The triumph of today: the life of Christ in me

These somewhat disheartening perspectives of the apparent defeat of the Church in time, and the power of the devil, could depress us. But let us not be overwhelmed by sadness. The triumph is already realized in us if we are Christians, if we have the life of grace. Christians who live the life of grace, who are aware of it, who maintain and develop it by an "exchange"[33] with God and through Communion, triumph unceasingly, for the life of God is in them.

Christians in China, in Shanghai, understand this well. Recently I received letters from the Carmelites in Shanghai who had suffered persecution.[34] What welled up in their souls was gratitude for having been united to the sufferings of Christ, in those villages under Communist control, and to Christ's apparent defeat. These Carmelites wrote to me: "We have left our native Sisters down there." But the only sadness the latter felt was this: "How can we spend twenty, thirty years without Communion? [...] But then, if God wills it, we will stay."

These souls experienced under persecution an inner triumph and the certitude of the presence of the Holy Spirit in their souls, of the life of Christ. And this life, which continually increases in souls, will enable them to hold fast under the strain, not only in face of threats but also under the psychological and physical torments which will be their lot.

Let us try ourselves, if not to reach such heights as these, at least to be aware of this life of God within us, to develop it, and to seek our certitude and assurance in it.... In this way, may we always advance, in spite of the temptations of the devil and external pressures, so that this life of God within us will triumph as we work to the best of our ability for the upbuilding of the mystical Body of Christ.

Notes

[1] 2 Cor 12:9.
[2] 2 Cor 12:10.
[3] Cf. Lk 2:34.
[4] Cf. Mt 3:2.
[5] Cf. in particular Mt 20:23ff.
[6] Cf. Lk 22:24.
[7] Jn 18:37.
[8] Jn 19:9.
[9] Jn 18:36.
[10] Cf. Ac 1:6.
[11] Lk 1:32-33.
[12] Mt 13:31.
[13] Cf. Eph 3:1-12.
[14] Cf. in particular Eph 1:3-10.
[15] Col 1:19-20.

[16] Eph 1:22-23.

[17] Cf. Eph 1:23; Col 2:10; 3:11.

[18] Cf. Eph 4:13.

[19] Cf. Mt 13:24-30.

[20] St. John of the Cross, *The Dark Night of the Soul*, II, 23, 384-385.

[21] Cf. Lk 4:1.

[22] Cf. Mt 4:1-11.

[23] Cf. Mt 12:43-45.

[24] Cf. Jn 6:70 and 13:2.

[25] Lk 22:53.

[26] Cf. Lk 22:44.

[27] Cf. in particular Jn 12:31; 14:30.

[28] Lk 18:8.

[29] Mt 24:12-13.

[30] Mt 24:22.

[31] Cf. Mt 26:64.

[32] Cf. in particular 1 Th 4:16ff.

[33] "Exchange" here signifies "prayer" according to the definition of St. Teresa of Avila: "Prayer is an exchange of friendship in which one speaks alone with God who one knows loves one" (*Life*, ch. 8, 67).

[34] Cf. in this connection passages of letters published in *Père d'une multitude* [*Father of a multitude*], Sarment-Fayard 1988, 158, 160.

The Primacy of the Holy Spirit

The apostolate has for its end the building up of the Mystical Body of Christ, the whole Christ, that is, the Church. In this work it encounters the radical opposition of the devil and the kingdom of Satan. The prince of this world, as he was recognized and proclaimed by Christ Jesus, wins apparent victories in this struggle over the building up of the Mystical Body.

I — THE LIVING PRESENCE OF THE HOLY SPIRIT

Now, Jesus has promised: "I will send you the Paraclete, the Spirit, who will be your consoler, your strength. He will enlighten you and will remind you of all that I have taught you, and will tell you other things besides."[1] The Holy Spirit prolongs and completes the mission of Christ Jesus, the Word incarnate, in this world.

We already encounter the Holy Spirit in the Old Testament, although there the distinction of

Persons in the Blessed Trinity does not appear explicitly. But it is very clear in the New Testament.

Jesus led by the Spirit

On the day of the Annunciation, when the Incarnation takes place, the archangel Gabriel announces to the Virgin Mary that the Holy Spirit will come within her and will overshadow her.[2] The Holy Spirit envelops her and effects within her the mystery of the Incarnation.

When Jesus Himself enters upon His public life, He presents Himself to John the Baptist to be baptized. The Holy Spirit descends upon Christ in the form of a dove, and it is by this sign that John the Baptist recognizes Him. "He on whom you see the Spirit descend and remain, this is the Messiah, the one whom I have sent."[3] Then, the Gospel tells us, Jesus is led *by the Spirit* into the desert.[4]

Jesus, when He has begun His public life, goes to Nazareth and reads the sacred word in the synagogue. He opens the Holy Scriptures and providentially comes upon the passage in Isaiah which proclaims that the Messiah will be filled with the Holy Spirit: "*Spiritus Domini super me*, the Spirit of God will rest upon me." To His fellow compatriots of Nazareth, who know Him and take Him to be simply the son of Joseph the carpenter, Jesus says: "Today this word is fulfilled in me, I am He of whom it is said that the Holy Spirit will rest on Him."[5] And throughout His life, Jesus is led by the Holy Spirit.

At the birth of the Church

The Holy Spirit begins His mission. As we saw above, Jesus, before ascending into heaven, said to the Apostles, "Do not leave Jerusalem, because I am going to send you the Holy Spirit. Do not go forth, do not begin your mission before the Holy Spirit shall have come upon you."[6]

On the day of Pentecost the Holy Spirit descends upon the Apostles. There is a manifestation, an outward theophany in fire and thunder. The Holy Spirit descends upon the Apostles and transforms them completely. He takes possession of them. The Church is already founded but the Holy Spirit, in a visible and sensible manner, takes possession of it and begins His external work in descending upon the Apostles. Peter immediately starts to speak, and his preaching works conversions at once.[7]

The Holy Spirit will manifest Himself, as we read in the Acts of the Apostles, in a visible way in the early Church. He gives Himself anew to the faithful, somewhat as on the day of Pentecost. They are baptized and receive the Holy Spirit.[8] It is the Holy Spirit who makes perfect Christians.

The Christian indwelt by the Spirit

What is the effect of this descent of the Holy Spirit? First, the Holy Spirit descends into souls. The apostle St. Paul has explained the Holy Spirit's action in souls very well. The grace of God, the divine life which unites us to Christ, this life of Christ which is given to us, is "poured into our souls by the Holy Spirit" and this is effected, adds St. Paul, by the Holy Spirit "who is given to us."[9] It is He therefore who does the work of sanctification.

Each time we receive this grace, even when we receive our Lord in Communion, it is through the Holy Spirit, the Spirit of Father and Son, that grace is given to us. The grace of confession, the graces which are given to us in the course of the day each time we make an act of supernatural faith or an act of love, are given to us by the Holy Spirit who is at work within us. The entire work of our sanctification is effected by Him and attributed to Him.

Furthermore, this Holy Spirit dwells personally in our soul. We are temples of the Holy Spirit. What is a soul? St. Teresa tells us: The soul is but a casket, a dwelling place. The Guest in this dwelling, the Guest for whom it is made, is the Holy Spirit.[10] So there is within us a real, living presence of the Holy Spirit. The soul is a small thing, it seems. It is but a casket in comparison with this Holy Spirit, who is like the soul of our soul, the life, the flowing source, and the sun of our soul.

These truths are very familiar to us, but our knowledge of them is not as vital, and as lived, as it was for the first Christians. When we read the letters of the apostle St. Paul and look for the difference between a Christian and a pagan, it stands out very clearly. What distinguishes the Christian from the pagan is this indwelling of the Holy Spirit.

The Christian is indwelt by the Holy Spirit. In our day we would be tempted to distinguish Christians by other characteristics. Christians, we might say, can be distinguished by their outward virtues, or by the joy shining in their faces, or some other such thing. Here the apostle St. Paul makes only one distinction: the indwelling of the Holy Spirit.

Each time he wishes to lay down a moral precept, whether it concerns the respect we owe to our bodies or our relationship with our neighbors, St. Paul always returns to this fundamental truth. Respect your body because it is the temple of the Holy Spirit[11]; respect your neighbor because your neighbor, every Christian, is holy.[12] We may be holy because of our own personal virtues, according to the measure of our grace, but we are holy primarily because we are indwelt by God, by the Holy Spirit.

This Holy Spirit dwells in our souls. I have not spoken in detail of His action. This would include a discussion of His role in the practice of the virtues, and above all in the exercise of the gifts of the Holy Spirit.[13] Let it suffice here for me to say that this presence of the Holy Spirit in our souls is an active presence. The Holy Spirit is a hearth, a sun which continually sends forth its rays. He is a flowing fountain. He is the life of our soul, the soul of our soul, the great reality of our soul.

Vital principle of the Church

This real indwelling, this living presence of the Holy Spirit in our souls, is paralleled by the living presence of the Holy Spirit in the Church. In his encyclical *Mystici Corporis* Pope Pius XII said that the Holy Spirit is the soul of the Church. What does this mean?

The Holy Spirit is the life of the Church. He is its vital principle, not only in giving it life, but also as its vital principle of action. We might be tempted to limit this action of the Holy Spirit to a few quite extraordinary interventions. This is not the case. The Holy Spirit lives in the Church and continually animates it, so much so that the first Apostles, making decisions at the Council of Jerusalem, said — out of their lived experience: "It has seemed good to us and to the Holy Spirit,"[14] namely, that Holy Spirit who is in the Church and who guides us.

The Holy Spirit builds the Church, He sustains it, He directs everything. At each instant He gives life to souls and develops the Church. He gives light to those who are charged with directing the Church and also to those who must obey.

This Holy Spirit is a divine Person and consequently is infinitely intelligent. The Holy Spirit knows what He wants. He has a thought, a plan which He wishes to realize, and His interventions affect the slightest details of the construction and upbuilding of the Church. Obviously, we can see His action in certain extraordinary events. We find it in the overall life of the Church through the centuries. We do not see it in detail, but faith teaches us that the Holy Spirit is truly the planner, the architect, the worker who sanctifies souls. He is the true builder of the Church.

This is a truth upon which I need not insist further, but we ought to recognize it as a *living* truth. It is not a matter of believing in the Holy Spirit in a vague sort of way. We must believe in Him as a living reality, a living, intelligent, all-powerful Person, a Person who *knows* what He wants, who does what He *wills*, and who knows where He is going.

Christians, consequently — and not only those who have offices and responsibilities but all Christians — ought to live in contact with the Holy Spirit. Not to keep in touch with the Holy Spirit is to misunderstand the acting power, the true architect, the master, or if I may use the expression, the "patron" of the Church, the edifice under construction.

II — COLLABORATION WITH THE HOLY SPIRIT

Our apostolate should obviously be inspired by this fundamental truth. What form will it take, this apostolate of ours whose end is the upbuilding, the construction of the Church? The personal apostolate which we are to realize can only be an apostolate of collaboration.

The Holy Spirit is not merely someone whom we serve, a statue we honor, a great master whom we salute from afar, whose influence we do not feel, and who moreover is not interested in us and the work we have to do. No. He is the architect, the constructor and the builder. What is required of us is the work of collaboration.

Let us try to analyze this collaboration that defines the apostolate, and discover its characteristics.

Indispensable collaboration

In the first place, this collaboration is necessary. God the Father has sent His Son, our Lord tells us. "As the Father has sent me, even so I send you."[15] Jesus ascends to heaven and leaves His Apostles to build the Church. He asks them to work, and this work — first the work of the Apostles and then the work of every apostle, every Christian — in the building of the Church, is a necessary and indispensable collaboration.

Let us not think that the Holy Spirit will take care of everything alone. He needs us. It is one of the laws of God's action, even on the supernatural plane, to do nothing alone, to act only with human collaboration.

Let us take an example, the most important one, that of the Incarnation. The Word is to become flesh, to assume a humanity in order to live among us. It is a wholly astounding prodigy that the Word, a Person of the Blessed Trinity, should become incarnate, assume a humanity. Yes, God will become incarnate. A divine Person, the second Person, will assume a humanity. To bring about this prodigious thing, what will God do? He will ask for human collaboration.

It might seem more fitting that God should become incarnate by forming a humanity for Himself. It would not have been difficult for Him. He would have only to say, "Let it be done," and it would come about. But no — He requests, through the archangel Gabriel, the collaboration of the Virgin Mary, an effective maternal collaboration in the full sense of the word.

The Fathers of the Church tell us that all

Heaven, even the Blessed Trinity, hung upon the response of the Virgin Mary and awaited her *fiat.*[16] What would have happened if she had not spoken the *fiat* of the Incarnation? It is inconceivable that this would happen, but the Incarnation would not then have taken place in the same way. God would have taken other means. Mary had the power to arrest the realization of the divine plan.

Our collaboration is necessary, therefore. It is one of the laws of God's action. If the instrument does not act, if it refuses, the work is not accomplished. If the priest refuses to hear a confession, it is possible that a soul may remain in sin. If the priest does not say Mass and as a result souls do not assist at the Mass and communicate, they will not receive the graces attached to it. If an apostle or someone with a vocation ignores the call of God, souls will probably not be saved.

This is a disconcerting mystery. How can God, whose power is infinite, link it not only in the natural order but in the supernatural order as well, to the will and consent of an apostle or an instrument who may refuse, when the salvation of souls may depend upon it? Yet this is the way it is. Perhaps, you will say, God may make other appeals? Yes, perhaps... but not necessarily. All we know is that God will build His Church. But He will take other means.

This necessity of our cooperation confronts us

with a responsibility. If we turn away from God's call, or even from some good work He asks of us, from the apostolate which He may require of us in a general way or in some particular instance, the good will not be done, a soul may be lost.

This is why God has placed charity within us, the love which is given to us, the life which is poured into our souls by the Holy Spirit. This life of Christ unites us to Him by living bonds, and makes us enter into His thought, His life, His desires. Consequently, grace itself makes us apostles, and this independently of the call which has been addressed to us and the mission which has been given to us. Here again, in the very grace itself, we find a demand of the apostolate.

Instrumental collaboration

This apostolate, this collaboration to which we are called — what will it be? Obviously, it will be instrumental. It is good for us to keep this in mind and to be fully aware of it. The only architect, the only worker is the Holy Spirit.

The Church is built up with the life of Christ, with grace. Grace, participation in the life of God, is "made in heaven." Man cannot create it. The priest can confect the sacraments, but he does this through his priestly power as a vicar, through the sacerdotal character which is given to him. He can only activate supernatural causes. It is not he who produces grace; it is the sacrament instituted by Christ. Our collaboration therefore will only be instrumental.

We should not think of our apostolate as our personal work. Even when we are entrusted with something for which we are responsible, our collaboration remains instrumental. The builder, the agent, the worker is the Holy Spirit.

We remain instruments. This is very clear even in the case of the priest, who in truth is another Christ, and has the sacerdotal character. This character only gives him the power of a vicar, that is, he can make the gestures of Christ, to which Christ Himself has attached fruitfulness and efficacy.

The Church is not our work. The spiritual work with which we are entrusted or which we ourselves may wish to do is not our work. It is the work of the Holy Spirit. We carry it out as instruments in the hands of a principal agent, the Holy Spirit.

In the conferences which follow, we shall draw conclusions from this essential and fundamental truth.

Human collaboration, intelligent and free

Our collaboration is instrumental, but nonetheless it remains human collaboration. Here we are getting into a far more difficult question, a mystery.

In the hands of God we are only instruments, tools used by a worker to make something. Yet we do not abdicate our human character and capability when we become apostles. Our instrumental cooperation remains human, that is, it includes the exercise of our mind, our freedom, and all our human powers.

How can it be that there are two freedoms at work here, two minds cooperating in the same work, the same task of organization and practical execution? That is the mystery! And yet we have to affirm that God only asks of us a purely instrumental cooperation. Some pious souls, whose mysticism borders on quietism, would gladly say, "My God, I am all yours, do with me what you will; I do not ask to know anything about it." That is quietism — I might almost say, folly.

We have to act with our minds and wills, and God wants us to use them. He does not want a dead instrument in His hands. If modern technology standardizes everything and turns man into a machine, God never does.

He has created us as human persons and given us freedom, and intellects, and He wills that in His service, in the most delicate and lofty works which He may require of us, we should use our minds, wills and freedom to act freely and intelligently with Him. He wants free and intelligent collaboration.

So this is what the apostolate is: an intelligent,

free cooperation which will obviously include the full development and use of our faculties. Do these truths rest solely on philosophical grounds? No. Once again we find them in the Gospel.

Recall the parable about the talents.[17] Setting out on a journey, the master sends for his servants, and in accord with their capabilities as he knows them, gives five talents to the first, two to the second, and one to the third. He then departs. When he returns, our Lord tells us, he summons his servants and asks them, "What have you done with your talents?"

The first, an intelligent man, tells him: "You gave me five talents; here are ten." "Well done," replies the master, "since you have been faithful in lesser things, I will put you in charge of more; you have done well." He who had received two talents says, "I have gained two more over and above." The master congratulates him.

The third, who had only received one talent, perhaps because he was not too bright, or for some other reason, says, "Master, here is your talent. I have kept it safely." We know what the master says to him: "But I didn't give you the talent to keep safely. You should have traded with it." Then the servant says, "I knew you are very severe, and I was afraid of losing it. I said to myself: he gave it to me; here it is, I give it back."

The master is angry and takes the talent away from this man, giving it to the one who had traded with his five. Then he commands that the third servant should be cast into the outer darkness, because he did not trade with the talent which was given to him. "Since you knew I am a severe man, you ought to have traded with your talent, and gained some increase."

The Kingdom of God is like this master who gives out the talents. We have to trade with them, that is, we must use our minds and every means at our disposal in the apostolic work given to us by the master.

Finally, the collaboration required of us should extend not only to the use of our personal capabilities, but even to technology and other external means at our disposal. In the reproaches made to the servant who did not trade with his talent, the master says to him, "You should have put it in the bank." We should use technology for the apostolate. For the sake of the Kingdom of God, we should use modern inventions and all other means at our disposal.

III — PERFECT UNION WITH THE HOLY SPIRIT

We see at once the mystery, the difficulty of our situation.

Respect for God's rights

The difficulty consists in remaining united to the Holy Spirit and respecting His rights as the artisan, architect, and builder. The Church is God's field, we are God's field. My Father works, says our Lord.[18] He is the one who works, makes fruitful, acts, gives rain to the just and unjust.[19] He does everything. He is the builder.

How shall we respect these rights of God, rights of the architect who has conceived and elaborated the plan of the work to be accomplished, and who has not only determined all the details but who wishes to carry them out Himself? And how shall we at the same time perform intelligent work? The problem appears very difficult when we consider it only on the intellectual plane, but at the spiritual level I believe it can be easily resolved.

To live united to the Holy Spirit

Since the collaboration which we owe to the Holy Spirit, the apostolate we are to carry out, is necessary and is imposed upon us, the chief requisite is our *perfect union with God.*

God the Holy Spirit is building the Church. He knows its measure, the proportions of this Mystical Body of Christ which we are constructing and which is in the process of growing. He knows its symmetry, dimensions, and details. We should therefore submit ourselves to His plan. How do we submit ourselves? By respecting His plan and by uniting ourselves to Him. Since it is He who does all, and we are but instruments, the apostolate requires in the very first place our union with the Holy Spirit.

Do we not often separate the apostolate from our interior life, our spiritual life, and our union with God? A person may say, "Union with God is fine for mystics, since they live in cloisters, but as for me, I have work to do."

If we work without being united to God, we are not respecting the Holy Spirit, we are not respecting the rights of God, and our work is fruitless. Can God make the work we do fruitful? Yes, He is free to do anything. He even uses the devil. Consequently He is able to use us for some useful work, even to accomplish some good. But we will not be sanctified through our part in this supernatural work of the apostolate, because we have not respected the rights of God.

From the point of view of effectiveness, God, since He makes use of everything, even the devil, for the building of His Church, can make use of us. But we are not true instruments of God. We are instruments in spite of ourselves, not altogether perhaps, because we do love Him, but we are not true apostles.

Union with God is an *essential* condition for the apostolate. A carpenter who wishes to use a hammer begins by picking it up. But if its handle is broken he simply doesn't use it. So let us not separate union with God from the apostolate. This is an error and runs counter to the Gospel and to theology.

This union with God is not simply a vague sort of union. We just now touched upon the problem: the difficulty of collaborating with God, of carrying out His thought, of being just an instrument, not only in great matters but even in details. This union must be profound. We spoke of the collaboration between two minds, the mind of God and ours; between two wills, the will of God and ours. How can this collaboration be perfected except by a *fusion* of the two minds, the two wills?

We already have an inkling of the requirements of the apostolate. The perfect apostle, of whom we spoke in the last conference, is someone whose will is completely united, in a way we might call almost permanent and habitual, by a very high degree of charity, to the will and mind of God. This degree of grace is so lofty that God is living in this soul. He is its master and can move it as if He were the soul's mind and will. Consequently, He abides in its depths. He holds sway in this soul, controls the activities of its faculties and can move them as He wishes, this way and that.

The apostolate therefore requires perfect union with God. The first duty of the apostle is not to work, and learn techniques, but to be an instrument of God.

Perfecting the instrument for God

The second duty of the apostle flows from what we have just said. Since this instrument still has its own activity, and since the work will be all the better done as the instrument is more perfect, it is also necessary that the apostle perfect the faculties to be placed at God's disposal. When we wish to use a saw or a knife, our work will be all the better if the tool is well sharpened.

We should not say, "God is powerful enough, He can manage everything." God arranges things as He wishes, but it is our duty to dispose ourselves and so to offer Him as perfect an instrument as possible from the supernatural, intellectual, and even physical point of view. Then the instrument will be truly worthy of the hand that chooses it, the power of the God who wishes to use it.

Furthermore, it is necessary that the instrument in turn make use of techniques. We must not subscribe to quietism, which we were speaking of just now, and say, "God will manage things, He is powerful enough; there is no need for me to use modern inventions in my apostolic work. God can take the place of these things." Yes, God can, but He does not do it. It is up to the instrument, the apostle, to use all available natural means. We must each do our utmost in carrying out the apostolate.

IV — OUR GREAT TREASURE: FAITH IN THE HOLY SPIRIT

We can already see some of the practical conclusions which follow from these truths.

As always, when we approach the realm of the supernatural and try to establish contact between the finite and infinite, the temporal and the eternal, God and His creature, the soul and God, we find ourselves confronted with mysteries, paradoxes, apparent contradictions. How to resolve them? By abandoning ourselves. This is where abandonment and faith come into their own, faith in the presence of the Holy Spirit who is in our soul, in the architect who dwells within us, the divine Guest who is the life of our soul.

In order that this faith may be living, continual, active, truly a force, it is necessary that apostles be accustomed to intimate and profound contact with God. When we read Church history we observe the people placed by God at the great turning points in that history to accomplish some great work in the Church. They are always souls convinced of the presence of the Holy Spirit.

When the Apostles set out to conquer the world, what was their treasure? It was their experience of the Holy Spirit. They knew Him as a living Person, and could say to the Christian faithful, "It has seemed good to us, to us and to the Holy Spirit who is within us."[20] That was their great treasure.

They possessed certain human qualifications, and they certainly used them. The apostle St. Paul had studied extensively and was a highly intelligent person. He was the theologian of Christianity. Those with lesser talents accomplished external works which may have seemed less important. But all had the same conviction that the Holy Spirit dwelt within them.

Let us make an act of faith in this Holy Spirit who is in our souls. The Holy Spirit is not a thought, or a reality living in higher regions. He is *Someone* within us, who is the Life of our soul, the living Breath of our soul, the Guest of our soul acting in us unceasingly. He is a living Person, intelligent and loving, who dwells in us. We should therefore resolve to live with the Holy Spirit and seek Him out frequently.

When we enter within ourselves to pray or to examine our conscience and attitudes, the first thing we ought to seek, almost the only thing, is the Holy Spirit dwelling within us. He is there as our friend, our Guest. He, the architect of the Church, the worker of our sanctification, is there. He who builds the Church, the great work in which He associates us, is there.

We do not ask this Holy Spirit to reveal His presence to us by another Pentecost or by striking outward manifestations as He did on the day of Pentecost, but to deign to reveal His presence to us at least by giving us faith in Him.

As our Lord says, rivers of living water will flow from the heart of one who has the Spirit and who believes in Him.[21] The Holy Spirit will shed His light on this soul. Floods of life and light rush upon souls through the Holy Spirit, but they pass particularly through this one soul who has, so to speak, opened the divine locks through faith in the Spirit.

Notes

[1] Cf. Jn 14:16; 15:26-27.
[2] Cf. Lk 1:35.
[3] Cf. Jn 1:33.
[4] Cf. Lk 4:1.
[5] Cf. Lk 4:21.
[6] Cf. Lk 24:49.
[7] Cf. Ac 2:41.
[8] Cf. Ac 8:14-17.
[9] Cf. Rm 5:5.
[10] St. Teresa of Avila, *The Interior Castle*, 284ff.
[11] Cf. Cor 6:19.
[12] Cf. 1 Cor 3:16-17.
[13] Cf. "The Activity of God in Prayer," 77ff.
[14] Ac 15:28.
[15] Jn 20:21.
[16] Cf. St. Bernard, "Homily in Praise of Mary," 4, 8-9 (*Breviary*, Dec. 20).
[17] Cf. Mt 25:14-30.
[18] Cf. Jn 15:1.
[19] Cf. Mt 5:45.
[20] Cf. Ac 15:28.
[21] Cf. Jn 7:38.

Presence and Witness

The Church is built by the Holy Spirit. He is its architect and designer. This means that the work of the apostolate consists simply in collaboration with the Holy Spirit.

What will this collaboration be? As I said, it is not my intention to give a complete description of the apostolate, but simply to insist on certain fundamental laws, especially those which appear to have been forgotten in our day. I do this, moreover, not in a polemical or critical spirit, but simply for the sake of enlightenment, so that this truth may triumph and our apostolate may be more effective.

I — PRESENCE TO THE WORLD

This collaboration calls first of all for a presence. God could have built His Church — a visible society, it is true, but essentially a spiritual one — by a purely spiritual action, by choosing messengers as He did in the Old Testament, or legislators such as Moses. But God did not choose this way.

The law of the Incarnation

To build the Church, God the Father sent His Incarnate Word. The Word came among us, made Himself one of us, assumed a body. He emptied Himself, the apostle St. Paul tells us.[1] Without renouncing His divinity, He hid all outward privileges and came among us. He shared our weaknesses, He grew as a child, a youth, a man; He knew suffering and death.

The Letter to the Hebrews insists on this perfect likeness which Christ wished to take on. We do not have a high priest, it tells us, who is unable to have compassion for our sufferings. He has known our weaknesses and sorrows, He has known everything in human nature except sin. He has even painfully learned obedience, the obedience which enabled Him to be our Savior.[2]

The Word Incarnate was first a child in Nazareth, then a carpenter. Later as a preacher He mingled with the crowds as a man among men. So much so that his fellow Nazarenes, seeing Him take the chair in the synagogue and hearing Him proclaim Himself to be the Messiah, did not want to believe it.[3] They were too accustomed to seeing Jesus of Nazareth, the son of Mary and Joseph, in their midst.

This law of the Incarnation, which was operative in the foundation of the Church, will also be operative in the building up of the Mystical Body of Christ. At times the Holy Spirit will act in an extraordinary way. He will act in souls through His light, His impulses. He will sometimes produce extraordinary events, miracles. Ordinarily, however, He will work through instruments, human persons who will incarnate Him in their own settings where they live and act.

Jesus Himself, before ascending into heaven, sends His Apostles. He has chosen and formed them, He promises them the Holy Spirit, and He says to them, "As my Father has sent me, so I also send you."[4] The word of Jesus is a word in the fullest sense: "You have seen how I myself have become incarnate," He tells them, "have mixed with men, how I have lived among them and shared their sufferings, work, daily bread, joys. Now you must do the same. I send you as my Father sent me. Go and preach to all nations."[5]

We might say, actually, that the Apostles too are incarnated in the settings where they will work. We can trace the life of St. Paul fairly closely through his apostolic journeys. We see him becoming a part of the places he passes through: Corinth, Antioch, Asia Minor, and then Rome. It is a question of a real presence, not a presence from afar but rather, to use the word we chose just now, an incarnation.

It has been the same through the centuries. The Church, who knows well her power, and that she bears within herself the Holy Spirit and His omnipotence, will nonetheless send her apostles and missionaries throughout the world. As soon as some new part of the world was discovered, the Church immediately sent her missionaries there. She wants to be in each place, and not only through a priest who proclaims the truth and dispenses the sacraments. She wants to be present totally as the whole Christ, the mystical Christ. She wants to be present with all her states of life, including contemplative monasteries which reveal her interior riches and her spiritual power.

At every moment, therefore, the Church becomes incarnate. She wants to be present effectively in all parts of the world. She suffers grievously and considers it persecution when she is shut out or driven out of a country and cannot be there as Church.

In our day we can observe this preoccupation of the Church to incarnate herself in the world. The Sovereign Pontiff himself, in order to "incarnate" the Church increasingly, we might say, does not hesitate to create new forms of religious institutes which will enable her chosen members to live the life of all Christians and even of all men.

Like yeast

This will of Christ and the Church is linked to a providential law of the diffusion of Christ's life, of His Mystical Body. How is the life of Christ spread? The Kingdom of God, our Lord tells us, is like yeast which a woman puts into three measures of flour.[6] Allow the yeast to act, and it will transform the whole mixture. But in order for the yeast to act it must be put into the dough, it must be present there.

As we consider the history of the Church we see that it is through this obscure, active, powerful, transforming presence that the Church makes her most beautiful conquests, not only the most brilliant ones, but the most beautiful and profound conquests. It is by introducing the Christian leaven, the spiritual leaven, through her missionaries and ordinary Christians, that she has transformed so many different settings.

Some time ago I heard one of our most brilliant specialists in Roman history affirm that Roman civilization had been transformed after the Edict of Constantine at the beginning of the fourth century. It became Christian not through the effect of the edict and the mass conversions which it occasioned at the court of the emperor or among his officers, but thanks to the gradual penetration of Christians in the pagan mass, and especially the Christian children in their schools. A *spiritual* action, therefore, was at work through this presence.

Moreover divine grace, the life of Christ, is spread particularly through the sacraments, which are outward signs of grace and produce it. A sacrament calls for a ministry. A priest is needed for the Eucharist, for example. What we find at the sacramental level, namely the outward sign signifying and producing grace, we find likewise at the human level of the Christian, who should also be a sign of grace and introduce it into the mass he penetrates.

This is how the Church spreads. When we read the Decrees of the [First] Vatican Council[7] we find that the Church herself is like a standard ever raised on high, and that this presence of the Church is the great apologetic argument for her truth and the great instrument of her apostolate. Presence is therefore necessary.

We should not think that the Church is spread only by spiritual means. Even those who have recourse to spiritual means such as prayer and sacrifice should also utilize a certain physical presence. This is what we often tell our Carmelites. But, they will say, we can pray in Europe for the pagans in the Far East.... They can do this, certainly, and St. Thérèse of the Child Jesus did it. This is how she became the Patroness of the missions. But even this prayer requires the work that goes into establishing and maintaining contemplative monasteries.

This is a law which is affirmed today in many situations, and it is rightly insisted upon.

II — THE WITNESS OF HOLINESS

It seems to me, however, that it is good to explain this law, for a certain ambiguity can arise on the subject. I should like to devote the second part of this conference to clarifying the nature of this presence.

In order for Christian presence to be truly efficacious, it must be a witness. A presence that is not a witness would be of small value, and could even be dangerous.[8]

Let us look at the life of our Lord. Why did He come to earth? He tells us Himself: to bear witness to the truth. He affirms this in various conversations, particularly with Nicodemus.[9] As Son of God, He has come to bear witness to what God is. He is the Word, the Son of God. He has come into this world to tell us about heaven, about the nature of God and His intimate life.

Christ comes to bear witness to the truth by His word, His teaching, and His works. He tells the scribes and Pharisees: "If you do not believe my words, at least believe in the works I do."[10] I bear witness by my works and by what I am, to the truth of my word.

Every presence, to be effective, must also be a witness. The Apostles understood this very well, and we find in Peter's first discourse after Pentecost[11] this testimony: "We are witnesses," he says. Witnesses of what? Of the great fact at the foundation of Christianity: the resurrection of Christ. "This Christ whom you condemned and crucified has risen, and we are His witnesses."

The Apostles took pride only in the fact that they were witnesses, faithful to the word of Christ Himself: "You will be my witnesses in Judea, in Galilee, and to the ends of the earth."[12] They were charged to bear witness. Presence should therefore be a witness. And in order that this witness of the apostle may be truly efficacious, what is needed? What can we, what should we demand of this witness?

Mandated by the Church

First, the witness must be authorized. I am referring to the truth we discussed in the last conference: we said that the Holy Spirit is the architect and builder of the Church. It is He who builds it, who is responsible for it, who constructs it. Consequently all the workers who are called by whatsoever title to work in the Church must be mandated by Him, the

Holy Spirit, mandated by the Church, of which the Holy Spirit is the soul.

Christ Himself was sent by God. No one can take the priesthood for himself. Christ Himself was made a priest by God.[13] He was a priest through the hypostatic union,[14] bearing within Him divinity and humanity. He joined heaven and earth, He was already a mediator because He contained within Himself the two extremes, namely divinity and humanity. And yet the Apostle tells us that He was constituted by God "a priest according to the order of Melchizedek."[15] No one can take the priesthood for himself.

Every apostolate is not sacerdotal, but every apostolate implies a mission. Consequently we must be mandated by the Church to bear witness, if our apostolate is to be efficacious. The Holy Spirit can indeed utilize all causes, secondary causes, free causes, physical causes, to achieve His ends. This depends only on Him. But we ourselves, in order to call ourselves apostles, to have the right to bear witness truly for the Church and for God, must be mandated by the Holy Spirit and the Church.

We are aware that, as the apostle St. Paul has told us,[16] there are in the Church various functions, missions, organs, or as he puts it, various members. Each member has a mission, a particular role. We know that through our grace we all participate in the fulness of Christ's life, His divine life, as well as in all the privileges and functions of His priesthood. However, a special function is entrusted to each of us in the Mystical Body of Christ, that there we may carry on an apostolate.

We Christians each have an apostolic mission which comes to us through our particular life situation and the sacraments we have received. We may have several apostolic missions, and these could be multiplied, but every mission must come from God. We must receive our missions from God, and they are so to speak conferred upon us by the fact that they fit into our life situation and vocation. In addition to this, a particular apostolic mission may be given us.

If therefore we claim some mission or apostolate, and if this mission has not at least implicitly been given to us, if it is not compatible with our life situation, or if it has been refused to us by the hierarchy, by the Church, then we do not have the right to bear witness. Our testimony will not be of any worth.

This kind of witness might have a certain value from the purely natural and human point of view, but it has no value at all from the supernatural viewpoint, or that of the Church. It is not sanctioned by the Church and so has no standing as a mission authorized by the Church. We ought, therefore, to take the proper and necessary care to be authorized to carry out any particular apostolate which we may feel drawn to exercise.

There is no question here of holiness, or even charity or generosity. It is a question of authority. The Holy Spirit is responsible, and He works through the hierarchy, the Church. So it is necessary that we have the Church's approval in order to exercise our apostolate. Jesus was sent, the Apostles were sent, all missionaries are sent. Therefore we too, at our lower, perhaps more modest level, must take care to legitimatize our mission through the word of the Church.

The mission given us by the Church already assures in part the fruitfulness of our apostolate. With the apostolic mission attached to his priesthood, the priest finds he is able to carry out one or another apostolate. As for lay Christians, although we are not priests, we have what we may call a charism, to use St. Paul's expression. In the Pauline sense the word "charism" simply means a function to be carried out in one or another situation. The power to do extraordinary things is not an essential part of this concept.

Let us take for example members of Catholic Action who are mandated to work in their own settings — rural, working, or student — and to bear witness there. They already find in their charism a real power, a fruitfulness for their apostolate, independent of their personal qualities. Even the priest who is unworthy or in a state of mortal sin consecrates and absolves validly. Apostles find in their charisms a certain efficaciousness. Why? Because the charisms, the missions which they have received, truly make them God's instruments in God's hands, truly used by Him.

In order to verify this, we have only to read the Old Testament. The judges chosen by God to save Israel were not always holy people. Some of them did not come to a very brilliant end. We observe in them all kinds of faults. Yet God saves Israel through them and assures them of victory.

There can also be, and there will be in the New Testament, apostles, persons who have accomplished great things and were not themselves holy when at the height of their mission and works.

In the *Life* of St. Teresa we come upon a remark which is somewhat terrifying for priests, or apostles in general. She writes: "At the Last Judgment, how many of these trees we will see, these apostles who look like beautiful oaks, with branches extending far and wide, sheltering the birds of the air that take refuge in them; and when they come to the Last Judgment, what shall we see? We shall see a tree with its trunk eaten away by the worm of pride and vanity."[17] They have achieved some good work, but the work has not profited them, and may only gain them their condemnation.

Will any apostles who have accomplished

great things, performed miracles perhaps, be condemned? We can answer in the affirmative, for our Lord has told us: "On that day many will say to me, 'Lord, Lord, did we not prophesy in your name, and cast out demons in your name, and do many mighty works in your name?'" These people had certainly performed great works, even miracles, it would seem. "And then will I declare to them, 'I never knew you; depart from me, you evildoers.'"[18]

We should not conclude that this applies only to apostles who perform great works. The point I am trying to bring out is that the charism of the apostolate, the mission of the apostolate which is given to us by the Church, by the Holy Spirit, already insures true fruitfulness for the apostolate which we are exercising. It may therefore enjoy a certain success, but this does not necessarily prove the holiness of the instrument being used. The instrument is all we see. We do not always perceive the Holy Spirit. The fruitfulness of a person's apostolate simply proves that the mission given was divine and that the Holy Spirit truly mandated it and has brought it to completion for our sake.

It is well to recall this when reading the history of the papacy through the centuries. People sometimes like to find fault with the actions of various popes. There could be grounds for this. If historians tell us that certain facts are proven and true, we admit them. Yet this in no way detracts from the

Holy Spirit's action in the Church, nor from the legitimacy of the mission carried out and the decrees or decisions made.

Oriented to holiness

In order that we may bear witness — and here I am speaking, obviously, not to priests, or apostles with very special missions, but to Christians who, like all of you, want to bear witness in the situation where Providence has placed them — in order that this witness may be truly effective, it must be accompanied by works and holiness. I want to insist on this point, because it is the most practical aspect for you.

You are not priests. Consequently you do not have a sacerdotal character and power enabling you to pronounce sacramental words, to celebrate the sacraments. In general you do not have a mission either, or a charism properly so called. For the most part you have only received the mission of the apostolate. You have been told to be apostles in your own setting, to be the leaven which transforms the dough. Nowadays when presence and witness are spoken of, this is what is ordinarily meant.

It seems to me that we should insist here on the necessity of emphasizing the value of this witness. The generosity of many souls in our day impels our young apostles and also all who are concerned with the apostolate to bear witness in various settings. And it seems to me that we have not sufficiently acknowledged the value of their witness.

A presence which is merely a presence, not enhanced by the true witness of holiness, does not seem desirable to me, but on the contrary, dangerous. What is the apostolate asked of us in our own setting? It is more often the apostolate of example than of words. Of course we must sometimes witness to what we believe, to the truth, in one situation or another. But the main witness we ought to give is the witness *of what we are*. It is the witness of the Christian life, of the life of Christ which we bear within us. It is the witness of the Holy Spirit who is our Guest.

If we are sent into a given situation, it is in order that through our outward human bearing, the sum total of our human qualities and defects — which are veils, it is true, but which most people easily see through — that through all this people may discover the inner Guest who lives in our souls.

Let us imagine some Christian in whom the indwelling presence of the Holy Spirit is not apparent, and whose attitudes, conduct, and whole personality do not radiate the Christian life we assume is within. Let us suppose, further, that we observe in this person a lack of courage in testifying to the truth on some occasions. It seems to me that such a

Christian's witness would be vain. It could even be harmful.

In this instance, Christ is not being given. This Christian is leaven, but without life and transforming power. With hardly enough energy for survival, even that little is not being conserved. Such witness is of scant value. So, should it be given? I do not know. It is a good question.

This is the doubt I should like to awaken in your minds: does mere presence in itself have value? If, in our own setting, we are just like everybody else, if we do not radiate to others the life of God within us, what are we doing? One stone alongside another stone makes two stones. Is this of great value?

We do not expect a Christian, even a saint, to have no faults, or to be physically perfect and possess a profoundly penetrating intellect. We look for the kind of spiritual radiance which comes from the soul, which we can glimpse sometimes on a person's face, which shines out in attitudes, uprightness, a whole life.

We should be concerned, therefore, to enhance our witness. How do we do this, how do we make it fruitful? Let us return to the word of our Lord: "The Kingdom of God is like leaven,"[19] a leaven which acts on the whole dough, which has power to transform, to activate. We must possess this leaven. It is within us, it is the Kingdom of God, divine grace, the divine life which is in us.

In order that this witness may be totally effective, it is best accompanied by natural qualities which will make it loveable, attractive, captivating. But the essential thing is that this divine life exist in our soul. If the Kingdom of God is not within us, our witness may be an external, intellectual testimony to truth, but it will not be fully Christian. In other words, for our witness to be fully Christian we ourselves must be spiritual, we must bear within us the life of God. We must be holy.

Here is another truth we are prone to forget. If the Kingdom of God is like leaven, so also is evil. Today the battle, in all settings and in the world in general, is a battle between the two leavens.

We know well that where there is an atmosphere of opposition, truth is rarely advanced by discussion. Discussion and exposition are useful and have great results when we are dealing with minds that are open and receptive, thanks to their moral qualities. But where there is opposition, it is very rare for discussion to generate light and bring about conversions. The transformation will be effected by a far more profound element, neither intellectual nor psychic, but *spiritual*.

If we were to place an apostle, a Christian, in a given situation, it would be rash and proud to think that the Christian leaven would play its part if the Christian did not bear the divine life within. The leaven of evil has at its disposal a whole range of intellectual techniques and methods of gaining control over us. It works gradually, and stands an excellent chance of transforming us. Certain falls which we deplore may have been due to our not taking this law into account, or perhaps trusting too much in our own generosity.

Within the movement of the Spirit

What is our conclusion about bearing witness? I will simply recall to you a word of our Lord, or rather a Gospel scene.

Recall what happened when our Lord announced His Passion. From the Apostles who are so devoted to Him there comes an immediate protest. What does Peter want to do? He says he has a sword and will defend our Lord. And when our Lord foretells his denial, Peter will not accept this; it is impossible. Our Lord has to impose silence upon him.[20] We know what happens a few hours later. Peter, the head of the Apostles, denies Him. The hour of the power of darkness has come upon Peter. His beautiful ardor has completely disappeared. He denies our Lord to a servant girl.[21]

This clearly shows Peter what he is, and the worth of his generosity and ardor. But it also marvelously illustrates a spiritual truth for us. At the Ascension our Lord will say to His Apostles, "Go therefore and make disciples of all nations, baptizing them in the name of the Father and of the Son and of the Holy Spirit."[22] But this mission which Jesus gives them, this apostolic mission to conquer the whole world, is accompanied by an urgent warning: "Do not depart until you have received the Holy Spirit."[23]

After the Ascension, what do the Apostles do? They go to the Upper Room, and under the direction of the Virgin Mary[24] they pray to receive the Holy Spirit, the Spirit who will come to establish the Church, possess it and rule it, the Spirit who will come to take Jesus' place as founder and soul of the Church. And at the same time, the Spirit comes to take possession of the Apostles, to make them true apostles.

We should not see Pentecost simply as a brilliant outward theophany, or the Holy Spirit's taking possession of the Church insofar as it is the Mystical Body of Christ. We should also see it as His taking possession of the souls of the Apostles. This is the day when they truly become apostles, capable of bearing witness to the truth which they have received from Christ and which the Holy Spirit teaches them. They become true apostles because the Holy Spirit takes possession of them, because from now on they will be moved by the Holy Spirit; because on this day the Apostles have become holy.

If we turn to the writings of St. Teresa, we see

that this conquest of Pentecost is equivalent not to the summit, but to one of the higher degrees of the spiritual life, the moment when the Holy Spirit takes possession of a soul. Commenting on this St. Teresa tells us that the soul can, at this point, give itself completely to the apostolate.[25]

I should like to leave you with this simple truth: to be apostles, we must already be possessed by the Holy Spirit. It is not enough to be generous, for this could become dangerous as it was in Peter's case, since it led to his denial. It has been a danger for many Christians who have wanted to bear witness but who unfortunately allowed their fervor to grow cold and their spirit to be darkened. They have lost supernatural charity and perhaps even faith; at the least, they have lost their fidelity to their essential duties.

We have God with us, it is true, but there are different ways of having God with us. The presence of God in our soul is given to us by baptism. This presence is real, but it is not the same as God's possession of our soul. To be perfect apostles we need to be possessed by the Holy Spirit. A merely technical preparation for the apostolate does not suffice. It is not enough to learn about methods, communication skills, various ways of capturing audiences, or how to adapt to circumstances. Being perfect apostles means, basically, being possessed by the Holy Spirit, and preparation for this may take a long time.

"But we are losing time," someone will say. We are not losing time. We may be saving our souls, and we are insuring the fruitfulness of the apostolate. For it is not a matter of numbers. What difference does it make whether there are a thousand witnesses, or two? If the thousand witnesses are mediocre, they may witness against the truth, without intending to and despite their generosity.

Two witnesses who are holy will testify to Christ, for they will radiate Christ and the Holy Spirit whom they bear in their souls. Their action will be wholly inspired by the Holy Spirit, and therefore fruitful. Theirs will be the true apostolate.

Notes

[1] Cf. Ph 2:7.

[2] Cf. Heb 4:15; 5:8-10.

[3] Cf. Lk 4:16ff.

[4] Jn 20:21.

[5] Cf. Mt 28:19.

[6] Cf. Mt 13:3.

[7] The decrees of the First Vatican Council were promulgated in 1871.

[8] Cf. the development of this theme, 233ff.

[9] Cf. Jn 3:11ff.

[10] Cf. Jn 10:38.

[11] Ac 2:14ff.

[12] Cf. Ac 1:8.

[13] Cf. Heb 5:5ff.

[14] On the hypostatic union, see "The Perfect Contemplative Prayer of Christ," 164, n. 3.

[15] Cf. Heb 5:10.

[16] Cf. 1 Cor 12.

[17] Cf. St. Teresa of Avila, *Life*, ch. 31, 340.

[18] Mt 7:22-23.

[19] Cf. Mt 13:33.

[20] Cf. Lk 22:31-38 and parallels.

[21] Cf. Lk 22:53-62.

[22] Cf. Mt 28:19.

[23] Cf. Ac 1:4-5.

[24] Ac 1:13-14.

[25] Cf. St. Teresa of Avila, *The Interior Castle*, 348-353ff. and Father Marie-Eugene, *I Want to See God*, vol. 2, 647-660.

Prayer and Sacrifice

Means proper to the Mystical Body

The Church, the Mystical Body of Christ, has its means, its special requirements, its laws to guide those who wish to contribute to its upbuilding. Even in nature we see that everything has its requirements and laws. A chemical engineer who wants to succeed in any kind of project must submit to the laws and requirements of his science. A scholar must follow the methods and rules of whatever discipline he wishes to explore. The Mystical Body of Christ, which is a reality, also has its exigencies, which we may call its proper means.

It is good to observe and even to insist upon this truth, which is quite often misunderstood. People think that they can work for the building up of the Mystical Body of Christ in any way whatsoever, without considering the nature of the Church. In practice this happens particularly when we allow ourselves to become fascinated by the methods used in the kingdom of Satan. We have said that in this world Satan wins apparent victories which will probably continue until the endtime. And at times the sons of light,[1] who are working for the building up of the Mystical Body of Christ, become fascinated by the apparent success of the devil and would like to borrow his methods. Not his dishonest methods, of course, but they allow themselves to be too impressed by his techniques, and overlook the proper methods befitting the upbuilding of the Mystical Body. I believe this reproach can be directed to a certain number of methods or techniques currently being used in our Catholic apostolate. I do not want to go into detail but am just indicating the fact.

Christ Jesus has given us sure and infallible means for the upbuilding of His Mystical Body. We have only to observe what He Himself did, in order to know how we should collaborate.

I — PRAYER, THE ESSENTIAL FUNCTION

The first means is prayer. Prayer is not simply meant to satisfy a religious need or a kind of religious feeling. Prayer is needed for the upbuilding of the Mystical Body of Christ. Every apostle ought to pray, because prayer is indispensable in the providential supernatural economy.

To ask for grace

The Church is a spiritual reality. Granted, it is also a visible society, but essentially it is supernatural and spiritual. The Holy Spirit is the soul of the Church, its designer. He pours the life of Christ, that is, the life of God, grace, into souls. He comes to the aid of the Church.

Now only if we ask Him does the Holy Spirit act in the Church and does God ordinarily give His grace, or at least the measure of grace He intends. Even when God has decided to make a saint, to give His help, to perform some work; when He has elaborated a plan like that of the Church, which is His eternal design, even then God does not carry this out, or give the grace, unless we ask Him for it.

In the providential economy prayer is a necessity. In order to be convinced of this we have only to read the Gospel. We see that our Lord chooses His Apostles, calls them, makes them apostles and priests, yet tells them to pray for this. "Whatever you ask of my Father He will give you, because He loves you, yes — but pray to Him: you have not yet asked for anything."[2]

He promises them the Holy Spirit, He announces His coming in a certain way; and yet He asks them to pray, as they wait for the Holy Spirit, that He may come.

We need only see these examples to become

aware of the need for prayer in the providential economy. If we do not pray, we shall not receive anything. God will give the first grace, He can even work miracles without our asking for them; but He will not give the full measure of His grace, He will not build up the Mystical Body of Christ, He will not pour all the life of Christ into souls, if we do not ask for it, if we do not make use of prayer.

For the transformation of the apostle

Furthermore, prayer is necessary for apostles themselves. It is not only indispensable, as we have said, to set in motion the First Cause which is God, which is the Holy Spirit. It is necessary for apostles themselves.

Apostles are collaborators of God. We shall see this in more detail in the next conference. How can they become this, how can they unite their wills, intellects, and activity perfectly to that of God, if they are not united to Him? It is their duty to unite themselves to God, and they will achieve this through prayer, understood in the broad sense of the word, through prayer that is contemplation.

To arrive at this union with God, apostles need to pass through purifications which will destroy their imperfections and evil tendencies. They also need to experience the interior conversion which will orient all their faculties to God present in their souls. It is necessary for apostles habitually to place all their faculties and their whole souls under the action of God.

How will this work of purification, this transformation, this conversion of their whole being to God, this submission of all their faculties to the Holy Spirit present in their souls, be effected? How will this perfect docility of their whole being to the action of the Holy Spirit be achieved in their souls, so that they may be perfect collaborators? This work of interior transformation, which is not purely spiritual but also psychological, can only be accomplished through frequent and prolonged contact with God.

Apostles should normally be souls of prayer and even contemplatives. When we consider the lives of the great apostles in the history of the Church we see that they were all contemplatives and souls of prayer.

St. Paul was thrown to the earth on the road to Damascus, and immediately began his apostolate. He tells us himself that he spent three years in the desert of Arabia,[3] to begin his spiritual education anew in the school of the Holy Spirit. It was after this that he returned to his homeland, Tarsus, and was chosen by the Holy Spirit for his mission as Apostle to the Gentiles.

When we read his letters we observe a notable

difference between the earlier and later ones, between the letters to the Corinthians and Romans, and those which have rightly been called the contemplative letters, to the Colossians, Ephesians, and Philippians. The difference between them can be seen in the great lights the Apostle had been given in the interval, and the leisure which was provided by his captivity.

These captivity letters have actually been called contemplative. St. Paul was able to reflect on the great truths which he knew, and penetrate more deeply into God. He could now clarify and intensify the message which he was charged to pass on, and thus become the herald of the great mystery of God and the Church.

Finally, we think of the Fathers of the Church who had considerable influence in unfolding Christian dogma, and others who were instrumental in shaping spirituality in the Church and in guiding souls. We see that they all made sojourns into the desert, or at least prolonged their contemplation and prayer. In this contact with God, under His light, they were progressively transformed into the likeness of God. The action of the light of God made them true apostles. Prayer is, then, necessary to the apostolate itself.

To live by the very life of the Church

Finally, prayer is necessary to the Church. We could even say in a certain sense that prayer is the very life of the Church. Some time ago a spiritual work was published which had great merit from many points of view, and which discussed prayer. It sounded the praises of prayer, yet seemed to consider purely contemplative prayer as egotistical. The author stressed the value of the prayer that seeks God in the neighbor, with the unique object of saving souls and of charity to others.

This aspect is indeed highly praiseworthy. But it seems to me that to consider prayer only from this viewpoint and to deny the value of purely contemplative prayer is to gravely misunderstand the very essence of prayer and of the Church's life and purpose.

What is the Church? It is the Mystical Body of Christ. What is its purpose? The Church has no other end than to take possession of souls, win them over, place them in the light of Christ, and unite them to Him in charity, making them one thing with Him. This is the Church, the whole Christ, His Mystical Body.

When the Church has accomplished all this, is her mission done? No, it has only begun. The ultimate and essential goal of the Church is to lead souls into the life of the Blessed Trinity.

The Word became flesh. He assumed humanity in order to use it as a bait, a lure to attract us, and then, as the Church tells us on Ascension Day, to draw this captive humanity[4] after Him to where He lives, at the right hand of the Father, in the heart of the Blessed Trinity. We enter the Church not only to be its members, but to be united to Christ. Through our identification with Him we enter into the heart of the Blessed Trinity as children, there to do the works of the Word Himself.

Our vocation therefore is not only to be members of the Church, it is to be children of God. It is to share in all the works of the Word, to participate in His nature through grace, to share in His priesthood, His divine filiation, His light and His happiness. Our final end is to enter into the rhythm of Trinitarian life and to do there the works of the Word, the works of the Son.

We shall perform these works throughout eternity, for heaven is nothing else than this. Heaven does not consist in sensible or intellectual satisfaction. Heaven consists in seeing God and in being drawn into the movement of the Word in the heart of the Blessed Trinity. This work, namely, *seeing God*, will be our happiness in heaven. If we do not go to heaven in order to see God, it is not worth the trouble of going there, for that will be our work, our essential occupation.

Already in this world the Church engages in

this essential occupation, seeing God in heaven. She does it not only in hope, but in reality. Consequently contemplation, which means not merely finding traces of God in nature or His likeness and the participation in His life in a soul, but the contemplation of *God Himself*, is a work essential to the life of the Church. And it ought to be carried out by all Christians, in the measure in which they share in the life of the Church.

To refuse to consider God, therefore, and to contemplate God with the means He has given us in this world, namely the theological virtues and especially the virtue of faith enlightened by charity and the gifts of the Spirit, is to reject the essential function of the Christian. It is to want to reduce the Christian's supernatural and spiritual role to a purely temporary and indeed secondary one.

Contemplative prayer should therefore be carried on in this world, and especially by the apostle. Our grace enables us to share not only in a single function of the priesthood of Christ, that special role determined by our particular vocation. It enables us to share in all Christ's privileges. Everything of Christ's is mine,[5] all the operations of Christ are mine, and so I should exercise them all, according to my capabilities and vocation.

But in the Church there must be souls who exercise this function exclusively which we shall all exercise in heaven, where we shall see, penetrate, and contemplate God. Contemplative souls and contemplative monasteries are truly, as St. Thérèse of the Child Jesus said, *at the heart of the Church*,[6] not only because they follow her rhythms in their love, but also because the open eyes of their faith are fixed on God. To see only egotism in contemplatives — it can of course be found at times, especially in the first stages — is to seriously misunderstand the very essence of the life of the Church and her goal, which is to lead us to Trinitarian contemplation.

This is why the contemplative life, either pure or mixed with action, is absolutely necessary to the Church. Whatever the difficulties or failures we occasionally encounter, whatever the egotism we may note in one or another so-called contemplative who is on the road to perfect contemplation, we have no right to pass over the value and necessity of contemplation in the Church.

Jesus prayed

Prayer considered in this light is therefore necessary to the Church, and this is why Jesus prayed. When we consider the life of Christ in this world, and the proportion of time He gave to prayer and action, we learn something.

Christ Jesus came into this world to fulfill His role of Redeemer. He was not the victim of circumstances. He Himself arranged them with wisdom. What did He do? He spent thirty years in a hidden life. Not in order to lose time — there was not much time at His disposal — but because He wished to pray, to render worship to God. He wanted to teach us, by the proportionate amount of time He devoted to various activities, the importance of the functions He had come to carry out.

What does He do at Nazareth? He prays, He adores, He plunges into God. He bears the divinity within Him. He possesses both humanity and divinity, and in the silence of Nazareth, in His simple occupations, He constantly bathes His humanity, so to speak, in the divinity. This is His essential occupation.

When He enters upon His public life, He first spends forty days in the desert at prayer. When He preaches, He spends nights on the mountain at prayer. At the end of His life, during its most painful period, He spends His nights praying in the garden of Gethsemane. On the Cross, He prays. And the apostle St. Paul shows Him in heaven interceding for us.[7]

Christ, therefore, prayed. He was the perfect mediator, the Word incarnate. He indeed acted, preached, and bore witness. But above all He prayed.

The power of prayer

What does the Holy Spirit, the soul of the Church, its designer and builder, do in the Church and in our souls? The apostle St. Paul, with his marvelously keen sense of the divine, has clearly discerned this. The Holy Spirit groans in the Church, prays in the Church, and the Apostle invites us to listen to this groaning and to join our vocal and interior prayer with these groans of the Holy Spirit crying out to God, "Father...."[8]

All apostles, all saints have prayed. They have understood that this function is *essential*, vital for the Church. Hence we too have the obligation to pray. Prayer is one of the principal means at our disposal for working for the upbuilding of the Church.

At a time when we might have been tempted to underestimate the value of this essential means, God has raised up souls like St. Thérèse of the Child Jesus, who wanted her life to be exclusively a life of prayer. Drawn to action by personal attraction, she renounced its joys, she tells us, and immolated herself completely, consecrating her life completely to prayer.[9] Through the shower of roses she scatters, through the singular power which has been given to her, not only over individual souls but over the missions, God has shown the effectiveness of this prayer for the building up of the Mystical Body of Christ.

II — SACRIFICE, THE SOURCE OF LIFE

Having made His prayer of union, Jesus entered, after the Last Supper, upon His Passion. Sacrifice normally accompanies the prayer of union. Sacrifice should accompany prayer; moreover it is a special and wholly particular means God has chosen for the building up of the Mystical Body of Christ.

In Christ Jesus

The apostle St. Paul tells us very clearly that God has decreed to reunite all whom sin has separated in heaven and on earth.[10] Sin has thrown everything into chaos. It has deranged us by creating concupiscence, that revolt of the senses, and by creating pride. Sin itself is the cause of death, the separation of body from soul. The Word incarnate came into this world to unite all things, to be a mediator.

How will He carry out His mediation? How will He bring about unity? Through His blood, His sacrifice. It is in the blood of Christ that everything is reunited. This is the law God has ordained. He could certainly have done differently, could have restored everything by a simple gesture, a simple decision of His Mercy. He did not will this. He has invented, so to say, the law of sacrifice, of the shedding of blood. The blood of Christ is the blood of the New Covenant, the blood which reunites and purifies all things.

The apostle St. Paul has stressed this law of sacrifice. Throughout his letters we find the law of life through death. We are ransomed and brought to life by the blood of Christ, and the Apostle shows us how, by baptism, we already share in Christ's death.[11] He shows us how, particularly through the sacrament of life which is Communion, the Eucharist, we announce the death of Christ.[12] The sacrifice of the Mass is the prolongation, continuation, and renewal of the sacrifice of Calvary.

The Apostle shows us how in Christianity life springs from suffering and death. It is a law. Clearly, he knows well that this law is a scandal. It is folly, he says; it is a scandal.[13] We accept it with great difficulty. It runs so counter to our thoughts and all our aspirations that we cannot accept it. And yet it is a law of the Church's life. We must realize that life springs forth from suffering and death.

The Church was born from the side of Jesus, she came forth from His heart when the soldier pierced it.[14] It was at this moment that the Church truly came into being, through the blood of Christ.

Such is the law of the life of Christ. He Himself came into this world to bring us His message. He came primarily to perform His great deed, His sacrifice, the great action of Calvary. It was thus that

He saved us, became our Redeemer, and gave birth to His Mystical Body. He submitted to the law imposed upon Him by God's decree. He was obedient. He experienced how much it costs to obey,[15] being obedient even unto death, death on the Cross. This is why He has been exalted and has received a name above every other name, at which every knee shall bend in heaven and on earth.[16]

Christ's sacrifice is the source of His triumph; His painful obedience is the source of His power. It is because He was obedient even to death on the Cross that He has become the source of salvation for those who will obey Him. This is a law of Christianity.

In the Church, the whole Christ

This law of Christianity which Christ lovingly accepted and submitted to is also a law of the Church. We should not think of the Church as the whole Christ only in order to draw upon the "advantages," so to say, of this teaching. We also have to accept its "inconveniences." The Church is truly the whole Christ. She obeys the same laws and is governed by the same principles, since the Church is Christ. The law to which Christ submitted, the law of sacrifice, suffering, and death, is also the law which governs the life and growth of the Church.

The Church cannot develop and spread by any other means, she cannot grow through any other nourishment than that which presided over her birth, as it presided over the life and work of Christ.

Moreover, the Apostle tells us,[17] the soul enters into life through baptism, which is a participation in the death of Christ. Life develops in the soul through Communion, the sacrament of life. We receive Christ, and it is the living, glorious Christ who pours His life into our soul. He transforms us, absorbs us, gives Himself completely to us and becomes us. As St. Augustine says, it is we who eat Him, but He who absorbs us.[18] We become Christ. He who eats the flesh of Christ and drinks His blood has His life within him and becomes Christ.

This life which we receive is, however, the life of the immolated Christ. He is immolated upon the altar. His immolation continues in the separation of the bread and wine, and it is we who are to live out this immolation in the Church.

The Mass is the sacrifice of Calvary extended, we might say, to the Church. It is for us to live out the immolation. Communion should not be only a movement of union with Christ but also an immolation. Since we are uniting ourselves to the immolated Christ, union with Him necessarily means sharing in His immolation, His suffering, His sacrifice, and even His death.

Why is this? Because it is the law of the

Church's life. The life of Christ cannot be poured into us and into the world without suffering. Suffering and sacrifice are no accident. They are not misfortunes we might have avoided. They are a necessity. They are needed for the development of our soul's life and the Church's life in the world. Sacrifice is necessary for this. It is as necessary, by God's will, as was the sacrifice of Calvary for our redemption.

We must accept and carry out this law of the building up of the Mystical Body of Christ. This is not to say that we must look for sacrifice and immolate ourselves voluntarily. No. God will provide it. Christ Jesus Himself awaited His hour, the hour fixed by His Father. We do not even see Him practicing extraordinary mortifications. There would have been no reason for it, since He was innocent. He awaited the blows of misfortune, of providential instruments. And He accepted them.

It is the same for us. Sacrifice is necessary for the life of the Church. It is a means of the apostolate. It includes not only the things we cannot avoid but also the things we must accept.

In the apostle

The apostle will therefore be a contemplative and also, necessarily, an immolated apostle. If we want to work effectively with Christ in spreading His life among souls, we must use the means, immolation and sacrifice. We must, like the apostle St. Paul, fill up what is wanting to the Passion of Christ,[19] not that the merits of Christ need to be completed in themselves, for they are infinite, but our suffering and our sacrifice are still needed in order that His merits may be applied to our souls and those of others, and to the Church.

These are the proper means to be used in our apostolate. It may be helpful to study the action of the devil in the world, and to utilize certain means and techniques of his which we might call honest, to spread light and influence souls and minds, and to deal effectively with the masses. But the use of these means should not prevent us from recalling the proper and fruitful means for the upbuilding of the Mystical Body of Christ which have been demonstrated by Christ Jesus and the Holy Spirit. Techniques are necessary. Everything presented to us or recommended by the hierarchy as useful in Catholic Action or elsewhere is certainly necessary. But prayer and sacrifice are the principal and essential means for building up the Mystical Body of Christ.

The paradox of the Cross

We find it difficult to submit to this law. The apostle St. Paul tells us that the law of the Cross is a scandal, is folly.[20] It was true in his times, and is still true in our day. When the law of the Cross and sacrifice is proclaimed in a general way, little enthusiasm is aroused. When presented in the concrete and in its practical applications, it is always a scandal, even for those of us who are used to it. It goes counter to our aspirations; it wounds us, wounds our flesh. It conflicts with our thoughts and ideas. We cannot get used to it, yet it is the truth.

Yes, the truth is that the Church must suffer and be persecuted. The Church and we ourselves, Christians and apostles who want to work for her, must meet with failure.

I recently received a letter from the Carmelites[21] who had to leave Shanghai and who are now in the Philippines. They have been marvelously purified by the sufferings they endured in the Carmel of Shanghai during their resistance. These highly enlightened souls give, I am told, an impression of sanctity. Do you know what they said? "It was a fiasco, destruction, Calvary. . . ." They applied that to the Church in Shanghai.

Yes, the Church in Shanghai is enduring its Calvary at the present time. Communist power seems to have overcome and annihilated it. This diabolical technique, admirably organized as it is, has unfortunately victimized it. In what measure we do not know, but the field seems to be open and free before them. Yes, it is a fiasco, destruction, Good

Friday for the Church of Shanghai, the Church of China, in this hour.

Do not think that these Carmelites wrote in despair and sadness. They suffered deeply, yes, but at the same time they had a sense of victory, for the Church came into being on Good Friday, and she does so again in each of her defeats.

Two years ago I spoke with a Jesuit Father, the former superior of the mission in Shanghai, who had spent sixteen years in prison and bore the marks of it in body and soul. I thought I should console and encourage him, but he checked my attempts, and said, "No, Father, we are victorious. When we are able to return to China we shall see mass conversions. My judges told me that in China Communism had done what it wanted, and had met with no obstacle, or rather, only one — the Catholic religion.... We have influenced the masses, we have worked among the people. And when we return, we shall find the harvest ripe for the apostles who will go there."

The Carmelites of Shanghai said the same thing: "We have left souls there, hidden among the masses, Carmelite souls. They will restore Carmel in Shanghai and in China."

These are Christian words, words spoken, obviously, out of the suffering of failure and disaster. The missionary said to me, "I spent twenty-five years in Shanghai, and in a few months I saw all the work I had done destroyed, all the work of our Fathers during so many years: the University, their residence, and all the rest." Yes, it is true, there is great suffering in these disasters, and the Carmelites added, "We have come to understand, through these losses and all the destruction, the suffering of the Blessed Virgin on Holy Saturday."

And yet hope is alive. It is the Church that kindles it. The Church, and these souls, bear hope within them. They have built the Church, they have worked for her, they have entered profoundly into her, and this is already a victory. They have prepared the way for the future triumphs of the Church in this world, and also the triumphs of the Last Judgment, the triumphs of the glorious Church of Christ, pouring His light and life into souls, triumphing in them. This is the Church.

To prepare for these triumphs, let us understand that the means placed at our disposal are supernatural means: prayer and sacrifice. Let us ask the Holy Spirit who lives in our souls and in the Church, let us ask the Virgin Mary, Mother of Jesus, Mother of the whole Christ, to make us understand this. Let us ask them to help us to be apostles, all of us, through the external apostolate, in the measure of the obligations of our vocation, but above all through prayer, sacrifice, and daily suffering; through the acceptance of this suffering, sacrifice and defeat; and through the acceptance too of that final defeat, our death, the separation of our soul and body.

This will be a defeat, or rather the last defeat, sin's final victory over us. At the same time it will be our first definitive victory, for it will bring us into the heart of the Blessed Trinity where, united with Christ, we shall enter into the rhythm of Trinitarian life.

Notes

[1] Cf. Lk 16:8.

[2] Cf. Jn 16:23-24.

[3] Cf. Gal 1:17-18.

[4] "Ascending on high, he led captivity captive," Alleluia Verse, Liturgy of the Ascension.

[5] Cf. John of the Cross, "Prayer of the soul on fire with love," *Works*, 1183.

[6] Cf. *Manuscript B*, e v°.

[7] Cf. Heb 7:25.

[8] Cf. Rm 8; 15:26-27; Gal 4:4-7.

[9] Cf. Céline Martin (Sr. Genevieve of the Holy Face), *A Memoir of My Sister, St. Thérèse*, 109.

[10] Cf. Col 1:19-20.

[11] Cf. Rm 6:4.

[12] 1 Cor 11:26.

[13] Cf. 1 Cor 1:23-24.

[14] Cf. Jn 19:34.

[15] Heb 5:8.

[16] Ph 2:7-10.

[17] Rm 6:4.

[18] Cf. St. Augustine, *Confessions*, VII, 10.

[19] Cf. Col 1:24.

[20] Cf. 1 Cor 1:23.

[21] Cf. "Building the Kingdom," 193, n. 34.

The Perfect Apostle

In these conferences we have tried to consider some basic truths about the apostolate. We have seen that its essential purpose is the building up of the Kingdom of God, that is, the Mystical Body of Christ, the Church. This Kingdom of God is built in opposition to the kingdom of Satan, who wins apparent victories; victories which seem more and more brilliant, up to that final victory of his which will lead to the triumph of the Kingdom of God.

Furthermore, the apostolate is a form of collaboration, for the Kingdom of God, the Mystical Body of Christ, is built by the Holy Spirit. He is its designer and craftsman. By reason of its spiritual nature, this Kingdom of God has particular requirements which the apostolate, as a form of collaboration, should know and respect. Let us try to make a synthesis of these various truths by speaking of the perfect apostolate.

I — THE REQUIREMENTS OF THE CHRISTIAN APOSTOLATE

Who is the perfect apostle? Obviously, it is Christ. He came into this world to achieve our Redemption, through the building up of His Mystical Body. There are also Apostles whom Jesus chose and formed. To them He sent the Holy Spirit, who made of them perfect apostles.

In speaking of the perfect apostle, we shall fix our eyes on Jesus and the Apostles. We shall follow their guidance, avoiding all personal interpretation. And on the other hand we shall not hesitate, in light of their teaching and example, to affirm clearly the requirements of the Christian apostolate.

Each baptized person receives a mission

First, the apostle is one sent. Christ Jesus was sent by His Father, He was constituted priest and mediator according to the order of Melchizedek.[1] The Apostles were sent by Christ: "I send you. Go, preach to all nations, teach them and baptize them in the name of the Father, the Son, and the Holy Spirit."[2]

When the apostle St. Paul speaks to us of the Church, he insists on her unity: one Spirit, one faith, the same sacraments. But at the same time, in comparing the Church to a human body, he tells us that she has different members and organs.[3] This comparison serves to show both the unity of the Mystical Body of Christ and the diversity of its members.

Unity: every Christian receives with grace a complete share in divine life. Divine grace is essentially identical in all Christians. We are all children of God. This grace which is given to us, and which is the life of Christ, assures us of complete participation in all the privileges and functions of the priesthood of Christ. We are priests and kings with Christ.

But the grace which is given to us at baptism carries with it, for each of us, a particular tonality. Each of us is destined to reflect some divine attribute in a more particular way. The white light of God, which passes through Christ as through a prism, takes on a different hue in each soul. The Mystical Body of Christ thus displays all the beauties of the grace of Christ and we are charged, the apostle St. Peter tells us, to show forth the virtues and the beauty of "Him who called you out of darkness into His marvelous light."[4]

It is the same for the priesthood of Christ. We are all priests with Christ, and yet a distinct function in the Mystical Body of Christ is entrusted to each of us, to every Christian. With our own grace, therefore, we are given a special vocation and a particular mission. And if we wish to develop our grace in all its fulness, we must carry out this particular mission which forms an integral part of it. We must fulfill our vocation in the Mystical Body of Christ, our special share in the priesthood of Christ, if we wish to take our predestined place in the Trinitarian life.

Beginning then with grace, with the charity which is in us independently of whatever mission may be entrusted to us, under whatever circumstances, we are apostles, for we have a function to exercise in the priesthood of Christ.

From this fact we can already conclude that every Christian has the obligation to fulfill a certain apostolate. But now we need to clarify the meaning of this function.

This function is first fulfilled in the duties of our state in life

What is this function which is conferred upon us by the grace which has been given to us, by our belonging to the Mystical Body of Christ? It is not necessarily an extraordinary mission. There will indeed be some extraordinary missions included in the grace which has been given to us, and there may be some which are purely exterior to it. But as Christians we all have, we might say, an *ordinary* apostolic mission within our grace itself. It is important to make this point very clear, in order to understand the nature of the apostolate.

We often think of the apostolate as some form of work in the parish or in society. We see it as a particular commitment, something extra which we add to our ordinary duties. We call this our apostolate.

It is true that these missions which are given to us, these extras which we do during our free time, and to which we sacrifice our leisure, constitute an apostolate. We might be obliged, even in conscience, to undertake this kind of apostolate. But the apostolate considered in its essential reality is made up of *the duties of our state in life*. I insist on this point because there may be some confusion about it in your minds.

What will our apostolate be, then? Our role in the Church, ordinarily, is *the sum total of the duties of our state in life*. A priest has received the ministry of the priesthood. This priesthood, the commitment it requires of him, obedience to the bishop and the Church, may oblige him to fulfill one or another particular function or apostolate. But what is it that makes him truly an apostle? What is his essential function as an apostle in the Church? It is to be a priest, and to carry out the essential duties of his priesthood.

At the other end of the spectrum, let us take a married woman. She has received the sacrament of marriage. What will her essential apostolate be within the Church? Obviously, the procreation and education of children. Matrimony is not a sacrament external to the Church, which "legitimizes" a wholly natural act and sprinkles it with holy water, so to say. Marriage is destined to extend the Church, to create material temples which will become spiritual temples. Persons committed to marriage have as their essential duty the procreation and education of children, the building up of these material and spiritual temples which will thus enter into the Church of God and Trinitarian life.

When we examine our consciences and consider our duties, whatever the urgency of secondary, perhaps important commitments, whatever the demands made on us to carry them out, the fact remains that we must in the first place fulfill our essential duties.

When we come before the judgment seat of God and see the Church of God, the Mystical Body of Christ, in all its splendor and light, we ourselves shall be judged primarily on our fulfillment of these essential duties of our vocation, that is, on our destined place in the Church, and the sacraments we have received so as to fill it.

The stress placed on duties of Catholic Action and social duties of various kinds, which are very important — obviously I do not want to imply that they are of little importance for they may be very serious and even oblige us under pain of grave sin — this emphasis should never make us forget the essential duties of our particular role in the building of the Mystical Body of Christ.

A certain grace is attached to this mission

The mission entrusted to each of us in the Church carries with it powers, together with the ability to exercise them. Here too, often enough, we have connected an apostolic function with a charism, and almost unconsciously we have looked for charisms which would be extraordinary.

The apostle St. Paul speaks of charisms given to the members of the Mystical Body of Christ: roles of teaching, healing, etc. He mentions functions accompanied by extraordinary powers, moreover. In Pauline language charisms mean gifts, but they are not necessarily extraordinary. Charisms are gifts given because of their usefulness to the Mystical Body of Christ. They are given also for the soul's sanctification, but their principal purpose is the upbuilding of the Church.

This vocation, this role which is given to us and is connected with our grace, contains within it therefore powers which are sometimes extraordinary but which are always given. They carry with them the grace to exercise them. The power is given, like the authority, for the sake of our neighbor and the Church. Grace is given to us so that we may fulfill our role with charity, be sanctified in so doing, and may also develop the grace itself in exercising the role.

You can see very clearly from this the difference between charismatic grace and sanctifying grace. The second has the mark of holiness; the first is independent of it. People can do marvels and even work miracles, without being holy. We could have the gift of miracles without any increase in our sanctifying grace. God may make use of us for this. But with the former on the contrary, the grace which is given increases our capital, our strength, the power if not the fervor of our baptismal grace, and our sanctifying grace.

... but it does not suffice for its perfect fulfillment

This sanctifying grace, this particular grace given for the exercise of functions — and it must be distinguished from the function itself and from authority — is a grace insufficient in itself for the perfect fulfillment of the function. It is sufficient for performing the function under normal conditions, but insufficient for performing it habitually in a perfect way.

Here we are in the realm of experience. This is the way God acts. He did not act thus in the case of the Blessed Virgin. She was raised immediately, on the day of the Annunciation, to a degree of grace which made her worthy to be the Mother of God. But we see it for example in regard to the Apostles whom our Lord Himself chose, called, and to whom He assigned functions.

We see in the Gospel that He sends them out two by two to preach the Kingdom of God. He gives them power to drive out demons and to work miracles.[5] And when they return to Him Jesus says, in response to their enthusiasm, "Behold, I saw Satan fall like lightning from heaven."[6] He sees the fruitfulness and effectiveness of the powers He has given them. And yet at this time they are far from perfect. Our Lord does not hesitate to say to them, "How long am I to be with you and bear with you?"[7] They argue among themselves, are jealous, and each wants to hold the first place.[8]

We have here an example from life of an authentic function, even extraordinary powers, a call to the apostolate accompanied by the grace to exercise the function, yet all this does not produce sanctity, and does not yet make of the Apostles perfect witnesses.

A little later, at the Last Supper, our Lord institutes the Holy Eucharist and gives His Apostles the powers of the priesthood. Now not even these powers make perfect apostles of them. We see that indeed they are filled with fervor after having received the Body of Christ at the Last Supper. But the ardent protests of Peter and the promises of fidelity by the others[9] end up in a way we well know. Peter produces his sword and cuts off Malchus' ear, and this is a truly courageous act, but a few minutes after this he denies our Lord, and the rest flee.

Yet they are just a few hours away from their priestly ordination. Even the priesthood does not confer sanctity upon them, although it does give them sufficient grace to exercise their priestly office. This is true with all the more reason of the apostle who has a far more external function to fulfill. This grace therefore remains insufficient in itself.

Apostles who have received a function and a grace have therefore the duty of perfecting themselves. They cannot count absolutely on the grace they have received. They should not think that they have become saints and can throw themselves impetuously into the exercise of their apostolic roles since these roles seem to them very important and urgent. They have no right to rush in headlong without taking precautions and considering the dangers they may encounter.[10]

It seems to me that here too, and I need not stress the point, we are touching on a practical problem which has been resolved in a number of different ways in our day. Perhaps the falls we lament are due to the rashness of apostles who have received lofty functions. Very often they have sought an excuse in the fact that the task assigned to them was urgent; that souls needed them, that there was a priestly, or social, or apostolic duty to be met which required their total and unreserved dedication. They thought they could dash into their work, and alas the same thing happened to them as happened to Peter.

The Holy Spirit's rule is needed

We have therefore the duty of safeguarding our interior life, perfecting ourselves, and developing the grace that is within us. What does the perfect apostolate call for? Let us look at our Lord and the Apostles.

In our Lord we see a priestly mission, one of mediation, entrusted to Him. He must be the mediator between heaven and earth. In Him all must be reunited. This is the role given to Him. He is also the Savior, and He builds the Mystical Body, gathering all souls to Himself and leading them victoriously into the heart of the Blessed Trinity.

This function, in our Lord, is based on His hypostatic union. The function entrusted to Him is none other than the determination of what He is. He is the Man-God and bears within Him the two extremes: divinity and humanity. His humanity, clothed in this priesthood, is anointed with the divinity. He has therefore at His disposal an infinite grace, the anointing of the divinity, which makes Him the perfect mediator, the perfect witness, and gives infinite merit to His actions and sufferings. In Him there is equality of grace and function. His infinite grace brings Him to the height of His function of mediation.

We can already perceive the apostle's position by comparison. Sanctifying grace, held in a sense in abeyance, must parallel the loftiness of the mission which has been given. We ourselves shall have to acquire what was already realized in Christ by reason of His hypostatic union.

Let us see now what took place in the Apostles. They are made apostles, consecrated priests, and our Lord entrusts the Church to them: "As my Father has sent me, I also send you."[11] They are now in control: "All that you bind on earth will be bound in heaven, all that you loose on earth will be loosed in heaven."[12] These are the amplest powers, the most universal mission possible. Jesus departs. From now on, they must govern His Mystical Body, the Church.

But this function, this priesthood taken in itself, does not lift them to the height of their mission from the point of view of grace. This is why our Lord tells them, before setting out on the mission He has entrusted to them, to wait in Jerusalem for the coming of the Holy Spirit.

What is Pentecost? We can think of it as the manifestation of the Holy Spirit, marking His taking possession of the Church, the beginning of His work in this world. He takes possession of the work He is going to accomplish, and begins to realize it by extraordinary means. Thus He shows us His design. But we must also see in Pentecost *the Holy Spirit taking possession of the Apostles*. The subject we are presently discussing requires us to consider this aspect primarily.

On the day of Pentecost the Apostles are effectively transformed. They receive extraordinary gifts, but also an outpouring of sanctifying grace which is still more extraordinary. From this moment on they are enlightened. All the teaching they have received from Christ comes back to their minds. The Holy Spirit also enlightens them on other points, as our Lord had foretold.[13] They are filled with strength. On this day they are truly holy. They are seized by the Holy Spirit, and this Spirit moves them to proclaim the truths He imparts to their minds. The Holy Spirit impels them. He has truly taken possession of them.

Here, I believe we have touched on what essentially constitutes the perfection of the apostolate and the apostle. The apostle remains imperfect as long as only a mission and its accompanying grace have been received. The apostle who would be a collaborator with the Holy Spirit becomes a perfect apostle only when the Holy Spirit takes over completely.

It may seem that now we are entering the world of the miraculous and the marvelous. But this is not true. We are used to saying, when such realities are brought up, that these are mystical realities, extraordinary matters not meant for us but only for saints. This is not true either.

The organism of our grace possesses the sanctifying grace which is grafted onto the essence of our souls and makes us children of God. This organism is endowed with infused virtues which enable us to work and act in the supernatural order as children of God — as gods, since we have no other word for it. It empowers us to know God as He knows Himself, to love Him as He loves Himself, and this in all truth. We are able to render to God, when our love is perfect, the love He gives to us, to love Him as much as He loves us and also as perfectly as He loves us,[14] to love Him in God, since we are His children.

But our supernatural organism also possesses the gifts of the Holy Spirit, those antennae, the receptive capacities which permit the Holy Spirit present in our soul — present since He is given to us together with grace[15] — to act upon our soul, our intellect, our will which remains free, and to work there in so intimate a manner that our acts become divine acts.[16]

People sometimes limit this activity of the Holy Spirit through the gifts within us only to those extraordinary actions which we read about in the legends and acts of the martyrs. This is not the case. When we study Christian doctrine in the light of St. Augustine and St. Thomas — and there I would say that we are in good company from a theological point of view — we learn that the Holy Spirit acts directly in our souls to produce all our acts of virtue. Every virtuous act, they tell us, is an action of the Holy Spirit.[17] We have no right to deny this teaching on the action of God through the gifts of the Holy Spirit on the pretext that it has not yet been thoroughly researched. It is a matter of drawing practical conclusions from the common teaching of the Church.

Every apostle has the right to be seized in this way and should submit to it

This doctrine opens up to us some practical consequences.

First, God has given us gifts of the Holy Spirit whereby He substitutes in a certain way — I apologize for the imprecision of language, but I am trying above all to be clear — He substitutes, so to say, His personal, divine action, for ours. Or rather, He joins His action with ours so intimately that the action may be called divine. He has given these gifts of the Holy Spirit to every Christian and has not reserved them solely for saints or monks or contemplatives, for the simple reason that He wills to make use of them.

Second, if God has truly given us an apostolic vocation — I am limiting myself now to the essentials — a vocation included within our grace, conformable to the quality of our grace; and if the exercise of this apostolate, this function, is necessary for the development of our grace, in order that we may take our place in the Church and the place prepared for us in the heart of the Blessed Trinity; then it follows that God owes us the help needed to fulfill this role perfectly.

If He does not give us this help *immediately*, if He does not *at once* make us saints, if He does not *on the spot* raise us to the perfection of the apostolate and does not give us the means for fulfilling it perfectly *here and now*, it is because our Christian life is a warfare, and we must merit this grace. Providential economy rightly includes progress, progress obviously on the side of God, and the progress we must merit through our cooperation and prayer.

Consequently each of us, assuming that we have a function, has a strict right to grace, to the action and assistance of the Holy Spirit in fulfilling perfectly the function entrusted to us by our grace. This help of the Holy Spirit is possible without extraordinary gifts, solely with the organism of grace which we have received in baptism.

To obtain it, we must first put our mind to it and realize that our grace is insufficient. We must be aware of the divine realities within us, our vocation, and the nature of the apostolate, which is a form of collaboration. Our first concern as apostles, like workmen embarking on a task, is obviously to dispose ourselves to become perfect apostles, so as to assure this collaboration. Our first duty will not necessarily be to act. We must act, yes, but our first duty will be to act *well*, to develop our grace and union with Christ, so that our action may be truly good, truly apostolic, in other words, intimate collaboration.

It is not just a matter of having potentialities and lights. In order for our action to be perfect it is necessary that the Holy Spirit Himself move us, that He be so united to us that our action, while human of course, will be truly vivified, animated, divinized not only by the assistance but by the intimate action of the Holy Spirit.

In the life of the Apostles we see how our Lord gradually led them toward Pentecost. He had them share in the apostolate; then He gave them the priesthood. He made them pass through painful experiences, obliged them to pray, gave them the Holy Spirit, and even after that their holiness continued to develop.

The saints and masters of the spiritual life give us details on the union to be realized with the Holy Spirit. We find in St. Teresa, for example,[18] the stages we must pass through to reach this perfect collaboration. I stress this in order to bring out the following truth: the work of union with God does not have as its only end the realization of an intimate, mystical union with God. Its only end is not that we should work solely for the glory of God and the sanctification of our souls. This union with God is necessary, and perhaps even more urgently necessary, for the external tasks we have to accomplish in the apostolate. If we are not united to God our apostolic work will turn in on itself and be imperfect. It will be fortunate, indeed, if we ourselves do not collapse under the task, and in consequence lose the grace which we had when we first began our apostolic work.

To consider union with God as something achieved solely for the glory of God, for our soul's perfection, and above all, as was mentioned above, for the sake of self-centered mystical delights, is to misunderstand the value of this union with God. It is the Spirit's taking possession of us, union with the Holy Spirit, that is necessary for everyone and above all for apostles. This is precisely what makes for their perfection.

II — APOSTLES SEIZED BY THE HOLY SPIRIT

What will apostles seized by the Holy Spirit be like? They may, of course, receive extraordinary gifts, such as the gift of miracles. I would prefer not to discuss this charismatic order. God does what He wills in any case, and this is not an essential part of the apostolate.

Experience of the vivifying presence of the Spirit

Apostles living in perfect union with God will first of all be enlightened by the Holy Spirit. Our Lord said to the Apostles: "The Spirit will bring to your remembrance all that I have said to you… and He will declare to you the things that are to come."[19] And again, "He who loves me will be loved by my Father… and we will come to him and make our home with him."[20] This is the Gospel truth. "We will manifest ourselves to him." This is the promise of our Lord in the discourse after the Last Supper. All who are seized by the Holy Spirit receive an interior manifestation of the Holy Spirit, a manifestation of God.

This is not to say that they will have visions, but grace has been given to them to such a degree that it speaks truly of what it bears within it. This grace is accompanied by a quasi-experience. It reveals itself to the souls of apostles with power and vigor, and discloses the realities to which it is joined. This is an obscure but real mystical experience, which may take various forms.

In St. Teresa this experience will take the form of what she calls "an intellectual vision of the Blessed Trinity."[21] In St. Thérèse of the Child Jesus it will be an experience of "the Love which penetrates and envelops her."[22] St. Teresa will describe very clearly the mission entrusted to her. She will speak of it in detail and will be filled with reverence for the presence of God within her, for her mission, and for all the grace which has been given to her.

Moreover, this assistance of the Holy Spirit will vivify all the actions of apostles. When we see in the history of the Church the works accomplished by the saints and founders of Orders, by those who were placed by God at the turning points of history to undertake apostolic endeavors, we are astounded at the fruitfulness of their apostolates. This fruitfulness is explained quite simply by the fact that these souls performed a divine work. God moved them. They placed their powers at His disposal. While remaining wholly personal, their actions were also divine.

Identification with the praying and suffering Christ

This leads to an identification with Christ. Someone has said, *"Cor Pauli, cor Christi,"* the heart of Paul is the heart of Christ. We could say this of all the saints. An identification with Christ is realized, not only with Christ Jesus but with Christ who is the Church. We are struck by this when we read the apostle St. Paul. Generally, when he speaks of Christ we do not know whether he is referring to the personal Christ or to the Church, and he repeatedly uses the expression *"et in Christo Jesu"* ("and in Christ Jesus"). When he has poured forth truths which flow in a torrent of genitives, in language slightly crude but at the same time sparkling with light and powerful, he always finishes with *"et in Christo Jesu."* He is referring to a personal experience.

We find the same language of identification with Christ in saints such as St. Teresa of Avila and St. Thérèse of the Child Jesus. The latter says: "I don't know what I shall do in heaven. I shall be with God, but I can't think what it will be like, because I am already entirely with Him here on earth."[23] So there is identification, and it is realized uniquely in the order of grace, through its development, and, we might say, without extraordinary graces.

This identification with Christ which produces the fruitfulness of the apostles' actions attunes all the movements of their souls perfectly to the soul of Christ. They pray with Christ, in the light which is given. And this light is not just a general light regarding the divine presence in their souls. Given at its own moment, this light reveals both the eternal Church and the Church in time.

Apostles pray with Christ, and with the Holy Spirit who, according to the apostle St. Paul, groans within the soul with unspeakable groanings.[24] St. Paul's soul was so attuned to the soul of Christ and to the Holy Spirit that he could perceive the groaning of the Holy Spirit throughout nature.[25] His prayer was that of the Holy Spirit, of all nature which is in unceasing travail as it awaits its liberation. His divine experience, his seizure by the Holy Spirit, led him into the depths of God and the depths of things.

When we read St. Thérèse of the Child Jesus — I have been using these two saints as examples, but there are so many others I could use equally well — we see this same penetration of nature. If a soul penetrates nature, it is in order to pray and suffer. For the soul is truly, as Sr. Elizabeth[26] says, "an extended humanity" in this world. Christ in heaven can die no more, but there are still souls on earth, humanities which can pray and suffer.

What do their sufferings consist in? Above all they bear the weight of the sin of the world: "Behold the Lamb of God, who takes away the sin of the world," said St. John the Baptist in presenting Jesus to his disciples.[27] We can also say of these apostolic souls that they carry the weight of sin, some particular form of sin perhaps, but basically all sin seen as an offense, as opposition to God, the sin of their times.

St. Thérèse of the Child Jesus, in her cloister, said: "I bear the sin of my times, I eat the bread of modern incredulity."[28] And for her this translated into temptations against faith, a suffering which hemmed her in, cries and phantoms which haunted her in the night and said to her, "After this life, there is nothing." She ate this bread of modern incredulity with love for souls, and this is how she has become a source of light for her era.

Action and contemplation are inseparable

Apostles pray, suffer, act. In these realms action and contemplation go together. It is we at the bottom of the ladder who separate contemplation and action. Apostolic souls are always with God. St. Thérèse of the Child Jesus could say, "I rarely pass more than three minutes without thinking of God."[29] At the same time she acts, and what does she do? Whatever the Holy Spirit moves her to do. She was a contemplative, but if she had been an active religious, she would have been just as much a contemplative.

When we see the saints in this light, we no

longer separate the contemplative and active life. Exteriorly, people may be contemplatives or active religious according to the form of life which they embrace, but in themselves, in their real life, they are at one and the same time active and contemplative.

Here we have a sketch of perfect apostles, those totally united to the Holy Spirit.

The joy of divine achievements

Perfect apostles, making their way through prayer, suffering, and action, journey also in joy. Christ Jesus was a Man of Sorrows.[30] But He was also a Man of Joy, because He possessed the beatific vision. He contemplated the divinity which He bore within Him, and rejoiced in it as we shall in heaven. It is the source of joy.

At the same time He saw His Church. He told us this at times. When the Apostles returned to Him His heart exulted with joy and gratitude because He beheld His future triumphs.[31] Even standing before Caiaphas, when He was condemned, He saw this triumph of the endtime when He would come with His Cross to judge the living and the dead and assure His victory.[32] He lived in this joy, the joy of the vision of supernatural realities which He perceived, the certitude of final victory, the discovery and experience of this victory in the Church and in the world.

What is the death of the saints like? Let us consider St. Thérèse of the Child Jesus, a saint so close to us. She had told her sisters, "Do not be surprised if at the end you do not see me in consolation."[33] They wanted a beautiful death for her, on a feastday. "No, that is not for me. . . ."[34] And she said, "It is the death of Jesus on the Cross that I have asked for."[35] The death of Jesus on the Cross seemed to her the most beautiful death possible, and in fact this was the death she had.

Recently at Lisieux the Mother Prioress of Carmel showed me a statue of the Sacred Heart, and said: "It was before this statue that Mother Agnes, the older sister and 'little mother' of Thérèse of the Child Jesus, came on the afternoon of September 30th. Seeing the anguish of Thérèse, the sweat on her forehead, the suffering stamped on all her features, Mother Agnes left the Saint's bed of pain and went to this statue of the Sacred Heart where she loved to pray. 'There,' she told me, 'I prayed. I said, "Oh Sacred Heart, grant that my little sister may not die in abandonment and despair."'" It was the death of Jesus on the Cross.

Thérèse said, "I would not have believed a person could suffer so much,"[36] and then immediately added, "but I am in wonderful peace."[37] This is how she died, in anguish, suffering, combat, her last look lit up by the realities she already saw. It is this death of Jesus on the Cross that reveals her as a perfect apostle. Her death assured her victory.

Before His Passion Jesus said: "The prince of this world is already overcome,"[38] and yet He still had the whole struggle of the Passion to undergo. His last sigh, His great cry, was a cry of triumph, for it inaugurated His definitive fruitfulness, which was the Church. It is the same with the saints. This is how apostles enter upon victory, very often through a suffering which identifies them perfectly with Christ, or rather, which affirms their identification with Christ.

But the Church's life continues. St. Thérèse of the Child Jesus also said, "I will not be able to rest in heaven until the Mystical Body of Christ is complete, until," as she expressed it, "the number of the elect is filled up."[39] And this is indeed true. The saint continues her life in heaven, and just as Christ continues to act, to give His grace, and to pray for us, so the saints too, in heaven, continue their labors for the Mystical Body of Christ. There can be no rest until the Mystical Body comes to full completion.

Only when the Mystical Body shall have attained its full beauty, its full growth, will apostles have perfect joy. For their joy is found in God and in the Church. St. Thérèse of the Child Jesus expressed this again in her own simple, telling words: "In heaven, my glory will be a ray of light shining from the face of my mother, the Church."[40]

Notes

[1] Cf. Heb 6:20.

[2] Mt 28:18-19.

[3] Cf. 1 Cor 12.

[4] Cf. 1 P 2:9.

[5] Lk 9:1.

[6] Cf. Lk 10:18.

[7] Cf. Lk 9:41.

[8] Cf. Lk 9:46.

[9] Cf. Mt 26:31-35.

[10] For these important and delicate distinctions, cf. the last chapter of Father Marie-Eugene, *I Want to See God*, vol. 2, 625-631 and 637-643.

[11] Jn 20:21.

[12] Cf. Mt 16:19; Jn 20:23.

[13] Cf. Jn 16:12-15.

[14] On this "equality of love" cf. St. John of the Cross, *The Spiritual Canticle*, 887-888 and *I Want to See God*, vol. 2, 594.

[15] Cf. Rm 5:5.

[16] Cf. St. John of the Cross, *The Ascent of Mount Carmel*, bk. III, ch. 1, 309; and *The Living Flame of Love*, str. 3, 969.

[17] Cf. *Summa theologica*, Ia IIae, q. 55, a. 4; q. 109, a. 2.

[18] Cf. St. Teresa of Avila, *The Interior Castle*, part of the 4th Mansion, ch. 3 and 5th Mansion, ch. 3.

[19] Cf. Jn 14:26; 16:13.

[20] Jn 14:21.

[21] *The Interior Castle*, 7th Mansion, 430.

[22] *Manuscript A*, 84 r°.

[23] Here are the words of St. Thérèse in her *Yellow Notebook*, 15/5/7: "I do not see how I can have more after death than I already have in this life. I shall see God, true! but as for being with Him, I already have this here on earth."

[24] Cf. Rm 8:26.

[25] Cf. Rm 8:19 ff.

[26] Bl. Elizabeth of the Trinity, in her celebrated "Prayer to the Trinity."

[27] Jn 1:29, 35.

[28] Cf. *Manuscript C*, 6 r°.

[29] Céline Martin (Sr. Genevieve of the Holy Face), *A Memoir of My Sister, St. Thérèse*, 104.

[30] Cf. Is 53:3.

[31] Cf. Lk 10:21.

[32] Cf. Mt 26:64 and parallels.

[33] Here are the words of Thérèse, *Yellow Notebook*, 4/6/1: "Do not be disturbed, my little sisters, if I suffer a great deal and if you do not see in me, as I have already told you, any sign of happiness at the moment of my death."

[34] Cf. *Yellow Notebook*, 15/7/1.

[35] Cf. *Ibid.*, 4/6/1; 4/7/2.

[36] Cf. *Ibid.*: "I should never have believed it possible to suffer so much! Never! Never! I can only explain it by the ardent desire I have had to save souls."

[37] On the 24th of September she said, "If you knew what poverty I am in! [...] But in spite of its darkness, my soul is in an astonishing peace." (*Yellow Notebook*, 24/9/10).

[38] Cf. Jn 16:11.

[39] Cf. *Yellow Notebook*, 17/7.

[40] Cf. *Manuscript B*, 4 r°. Note that Father Marie-Eugene closes these conferences with the same quotation which closes his book, *I Want to See God* (vol. 2, 667). His masterpiece is actually as much a treatise on the apostolate as it is a summa of the spiritual life.